WITHDRAWN

Moyne Rice Smith

PLAYS

& HOW TO PRODUCE THEM

illustrated by Don Bolognese

*These plays may be used for live performances
which are not given for profit, without permission.*

To Deborah and Blackie
who always helped

CONTENTS

About This Book, 1

The Lady Who Put Salt In Her Coffee, 7 ✓

The Swineherd, 23

The Miniature Darzis, 43

Long and Short Division, 61

Old Pipes, 85

Chop-Chin and the Golden Dragon, 113

With All My Heart, 133

ABOUT THIS BOOK

To put on a play is fun.

The purpose of this book is to help you find a play and to give you some ideas about producing it. Of course you want a play which has a good plot and interesting characters; but you also want one which fits your number of actors, your amount of rehearsal time, your playing space and equipment. Here are seven plays which young actors made to answer their question, "What play shall we do?" You may use these plays as they are, or adapt them, or study them to learn how to make others.

You will discover that each one started from a ready-made story. This is one of the best methods of getting the right play for your group. Choose a story you like which has a good plot and interesting characters; then figure out what you can do to turn it into a play which meets your particular requirements. Many stories that will make good plays were written so long ago that they are no longer in copyright and are yours for the finding. The story you start with may turn into quite a different one, and you will be surprised to realize that you have in fact created your own play.

If you would like some help in choosing a story, making it into a script, organizing your rehearsals and your production, you may want to read the introductory section to *Plays and How To Put Them On* (Moyne Rice Smith, Walck, 1961). It will give you information about making and taking care of a stage, scenery, properties, costumes, lights, curtains. It will also give you suggestions about tickets, programs, posters, and so on. Some of this information is repeated here, but this book is intended particularly for those of you who are already familiar with the process of setting up a theater group. Each play has detailed notes which explain how to make the specific costumes and properties for that play and how to solve its production problems. But each play is flexible, and the notes suggest ways in which you can adapt the characters, dialogue and staging to suit your own needs. In general, the plays are twenty to thirty minutes long; but they can be made longer or shorter.

The stories from which these plays came are of different types, and they presented different challenges. A well-known fairy tale from central Europe, "The Elves and the Shoemaker," turned into a project of finding out about costumes, speech, manners and music of India, a country very different from the land of the original story. "The Miniature Darzis" may give you ideas about making a play from a folk tale of a special country you are familiar with, or one you would like to learn more about.

Another familiar fairy tale, "The Swineherd," became a stylized play which comments on what is false and what is true no matter what the country or the time. Because of its exaggerated artificiality, it intrigued our scenery artists.

"The Three Remarks," a story from a great-grandmother's *Supplementary Reader for the Fourth School Year,* turned into a verse play with Elizabethan music. We changed the name to the most important of the three remarks, "With All My Heart."

Because the story of "Chop-Chin and the Golden Dragon" took place in China, we decided to produce the play we made from that story in the style of the Chinese theater.

We liked the story of "Melisande" because it was a spoof of a fairy tale and because it had to do with old-fashioned mathematics when we were in the middle of the "new math." To emphasize the mathematical fun of the play, we named it "Long and Short Division." We wondered if we could figure out all of the tricky staging the play required; but we did figure it out, as you will see.

We produced "Old Pipes" indoors, but it would be a lovely outdoor play for camp. The notes after the script will give you some ideas of how to transplant it outdoors. The story reminded us of Heidi's country, so we suggested Switzerland in our costumes and music.

Mrs. Peterkin, the lady who put salt in her coffee, was an old friend of ours. We had read many of the absurd adventures of that lady and her family. Since all of the Peterkins already seemed alive to us, we thought it would be fun to make them truly alive on stage. Maybe you would like to try another one of their adventures, or an adventure of some other storybook friends of yours.

In addition to the specific properties and costumes for each play, some equipment which we used over and over again included a background drape, a number of platforms, several sections of movable steps, six screens which could be hinged together and some floodlight boxes.

Any material which hangs well will make a good drape to cover the back wall of your stage area. Stitch together strips of unbleached muslin or cotton flannel or monk's cloth and dye the drape in a tub of sky-blue water paint.

Our platforms were all eighteen inches high but were of different lengths and widths of plywood. The biggest were eight feet by four feet. Make them just like boxes and put short slits in the sides for handholds, so you can easily move and lift them. Small platforms on top of bigger ones makes good balconies and towers, and are good for thrones, benches, beds, seats, tables.

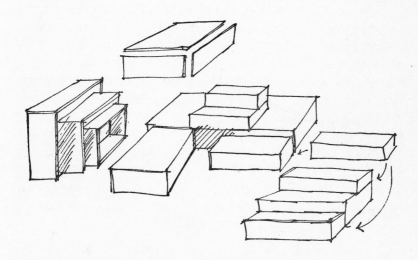

The sections of movable steps were the same height as our platforms, so they could stand against them. They are also useful as elevations on top of the platforms and are fine for making pretend hills to climb.

We made lightweight screens by nailing wallboard on both sides of wooden frames six feet high by four feet wide. We put

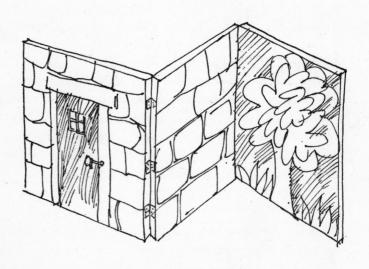

double-action hinges with removable pins on each screen, so that all of the screens could be hinged to stand together or in any number of sections. You can paint and repaint them with water paint for the scenery of different plays, or you can tack cardboard cutouts to them. Smaller screens, made the same way, make good hedges, rock walls, flower borders, and other scenery.

We made floodlights by lining wooden boxes with aluminum foil, boring holes in the boxes for wiring, screwing base-socket receptacles in the boxes, and attaching extension cords to them.

FRONT VIEW   REAR VIEW

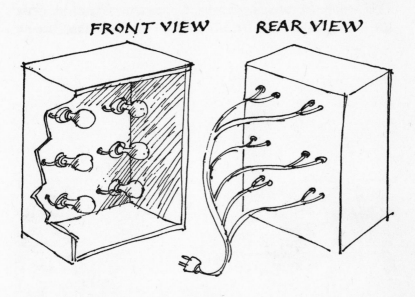

Stage directions are always given from the actor's point of view as he stands on the stage facing the audience. *Stage right* is toward the actor's right hand; *stage left* is toward his left hand. *Downstage* is toward the front of the stage; *upstage* is toward the back of the stage.

THE LADY WHO PUT SALT IN HER COFFEE

THE LADY WHO PUT SALT IN HER COFFEE

This is a dramatization of Lucretia P. Hale's first story in *The Peterkin Papers*. It was published in 1867 in *Our Young Folks*, a magazine which later became *St. Nicholas*, in which *The Peterkin Papers* appeared serially for many, many years.

Generations of children have become well acquainted with the adventures of the Peterkins, whose absurd attempts to deal with their problems get them into nonsensical situations which are solved by the Lady from Philadelphia, who has what the Peterkins lack—plain common sense. She is their fairy godmother, and her magic is logical thinking.

Julia Lockwood made this dramatization when she was thirteen years old. Many of the other stories would be fun to act. The stories have been reprinted many times in book form, and are now available in paperback. Read the stories and learn to know each member of the family. They meet many interesting people, so you might choose a story which has the right number of additional characters for your group. In this particular adventure the eight Peterkins meet a Chemist and his Wife and an Herb Woman, and of course the Lady from Philadelphia.

CHARACTERS

MRS. PETERKIN	THREE LITTLE BOYS
MR. PETERKIN	CHEMIST
ELIZABETH ELIZA	WIFE OF CHEMIST
AGAMEMNON	HERB WOMAN
SOLOMON JOHN	THE LADY FROM PHILADELPHIA

The curtain opens on the PETERKINS' *parlor on a late Sunday morning. At stage center is a small round table covered with a heavy fringed cloth; on it is a coffee cup and saucer. At right of table is a comfortable rocking chair. If you want to be realistic,*

*you may furnish the rest of the room. But all you need for the
play is the coffee and the chair and* MRS. PETERKIN *in the chair.*

(MRS. PETERKIN *takes the cup and saucer from the table
and rocks contentedly.*)

MRS. PETERKIN. How perfectly lovely to have my coffee all
alone in quiet. You can say all you want about how nice it is
to have a happy family. But it's nice to be alone sometimes
too. (*She hums a bit of a tune.*) And just to know they're all
having a happy time in the garden makes me happy just to
have a happy time all by myself. (*She sips her coffee. She
makes a horrible face, and stops rocking.*) UGH! What an
awful taste! What's happened to my coffee? (*calls*) Mr.
Peterkin! Come here quickly! Elizabeth Eliza! Agamemnon!
Solomon John! Little Boys! Help! Your mother's been
poisoned! HELP! HELP!

(*There is a sound of running feet.* MR. PETERKIN *enters
left, followed by* AGAMEMNON *and* SOLOMON JOHN. ELIZA-
BETH ELIZA *rushes in from right, followed by the* THREE
LITTLE BOYS.)

ELIZABETH ELIZA. Mother, Mother! What's wrong?

AGAMEMNON. Quick someone get the first-aid kit!

LITTLE BOYS (*jumping up and down*). A snake! A robber! Fire!
Oh! Oh! Oh!

MR. PETERKIN (*attempting unsuccessfully to restore order*).
Children, keep still! (*They are all now in a half circle around
her.*) Now Mrs. Peterkin, calm yourself and tell us what the
trouble is.

MRS. PETERKIN (*tremblingly hands him the cup*). Taste it!

(*The cup is handed from one to another. Each takes a sip,
makes a terrible face and hurries the cup to the next one.*)

MR. PETERKIN. Hmmmmmmmmmmmm . . .

SOLOMON JOHN (*sputtering*). Decidedly repulsive, definitely!

ELIZABETH ELIZA. How dreadful!

LITTLE BOYS (*all clamoring for a taste*). Let me! Let me! Let me! (*They choke, and* ELIZABETH ELIZA *pats their backs.*)

AGAMEMNON. Yes, there certainly is something wrong. Let me see. . . . Where have I tasted that flavor before? (*He scratches his head, as they all look hopefully at him.*)

MRS. PETERKIN. Yes, yes, Agamemnon. You have been to college. You can tell us!

ALL. Yes, tell us, Agamemnon!

AGAMEMNON. I know! Salt! That's what it is! You must have put salt in your coffee instead of sugar!

(*Everyone gasps in horror at the thought of it, then in admiration at* AGAMEMNON'S *brilliance.*)

MRS. PETERKIN (*thoughtfully*). Come to think of it, that's JUST what I did!

MR. PETERKIN (*importantly*). Something must be done!

MRS. PETERKIN. The sugar was right next to the salt and . . .

MR. PETERKIN (*shouting*). Everyone think!

(*Everyone puts his chin in his hand and thinks frowningly.*)

MRS. PETERKIN. They both LOOK the same. . . .

ELIZABETH ELIZA. Since Agamemnon's been to college, he should have an idea.

ALL. Yes, Agamemnon!

AGAMEMNON. Well . . . uh . . . everyone be quiet. . . . I have it! . . . No, I don't . . .

MRS. PETERKIN. Dear, dear, how could I . . .

AGAMEMNON. Wait a minute. . . . I know! Of course! Why didn't I think of it sooner? We'll go to the Chemist and see what he can do!

• 11 •

ALL. Yes! Yes!

MR. PETERKIN. Very well. He is a very wise man.

MRS. PETERKIN (*rising*). Little Boys, get your india-rubber boots. They're on the porch, all spick-and-span. I shined them this morning.

(*They move off in a procession headed by* AGAMEMNON, *who is followed by* MRS. PETERKIN *with her cup*, MR. PETERKIN, SOLOMON JOHN *and the* THREE LITTLE BOYS *herded along by* ELIZABETH ELIZA. *They march across the stage and off left, as the curtain closes.*

In front of the curtain from stage right the CHEMIST *pushes a cart covered with bottles and flasks and other laboratory paraphernalia. He is short and stout and wears a white uniform and an apron. He mumbles as he moves. He stops at stage left, where he leaves his cart. Then, still mumbling, he goes back off right and returns with a high stool which he places left of cart. From the cart he takes a cardboard sign, upon which is written a long equation, climbs on stool and fastens the sign to the curtain, climbs down, surveys sign, hunts for his glasses, puts them on, surveys sign again, climbs on stool, sits, gets pad and starts to scribble. All of the time he mutters formulas.*)

CHEMIST. Wait a minute . . . hold on . . . if the ultra violet rays break down the potassium INSTEAD, then the bicarbonate sugar and the yellow food coloring . . . Oh NO! That's not right. That's not RIGHT! (*tears his hair*) Dorinda! Dorinda! Please!

CHEMIST'S WIFE (*entering from stage right and coming to him*). No, no, no, no, no! I've told you and told you and told you there is NO MORE!

CHEMIST. But please, Dorinda, please I beg you, please, just let me have your wedding ring.

CHEMIST'S WIFE (*putting her hands behind her*). NOT my wedding ring!

CHEMIST (*gets off stool and kneels to her*). But, Dorinda, it's the only gold left in the house. And if it works, then you can have all the wedding rings you want.

CHEMIST'S WIFE. I only want ONE wedding ring. And I have it. AND I'm keeping it! You'll never find anything which will turn things to gold. And I'm going to keep the last gold we have!

CHEMIST. But, Dorinda, if I add just a little bit more gold, just a little bit more to my formula . . .

CHEMIST'S WIFE. I've given you my gold thimble and my great-grandfather's gold-rimmed spectacles, and my great-great-grandfather's gold-headed cane, and I'll NOT give you my wedding ring to melt with all the rest of your hodgepodge!

CHEMIST. But this time I feel sure I'll succeed. And then I can turn EVERYTHING into gold, and you shall have a new wedding ring of diamonds, all set in emeralds and rubies and topazes, and . . .

CHEMIST'S WIFE. (*Beginning to weaken, she takes her hands from behind her back and looks at her ring.*) Really, Halbert, that WOULD be lovely. . . .

(*Offstage right a doorbell clangs.* CHEMIST'S WIFE *dashes off to admit the* PETERKINS.)

CHEMIST (*jumping up and down in frustration*). Bother! Bother!

(The PETERKINS *enter in the same line in which they left the house. The* LITTLE BOYS *now have on their india-rubber boots. The* CHEMIST'S WIFE *has not returned with them. They march across the stage and stop, in their line, as the* CHEMIST *climbs back upon his stool.*)

CHEMIST. Whatever you've come about, I can't help you. I'm busy. And it's Sunday, and my wife was just about . . . where'd SHE get to? DORINDA! Oh well.

MRS. PETERKIN (*looking at her cup*). Whew! If we'd had to come much farther, all the evidence would've spilled out!

AGAMEMNON (*clearing his throat*). Excuse me, sir; we're extremely sorry to inconvenience you. . . .

CHEMIST (*picking up his notebook*). Listen to this! A to the second B Q squared plus one-sixth PI plus color equals . . . BAH! (*tears the piece of paper into bits and throws them in the air*) I've been trying to make gold for the past ten years. What do I get? Cement, mud pies, toothpaste . . . everything BUT gold! And what I need to finish my experiment is just a little bit of real gold for a touchstone, and my wife . . . and then here you all are. . . . What DO you want? Go AWAY!

AGAMEMNON. Our deepest regrets, but it's coffee we're interested in. . . .

CHEMIST. Got any gold on you?

MR. PETERKIN. Well . . . er . . .

SOLOMON JOHN. At home I have a gold-plated . . .

AGAMEMNON. No.

ELIZABETH ELIZA. Sorry.

CHEMIST (*to* MRS. PETERKIN). Aha! YOU do . . . I see it!

MRS. PETERKIN (*apologetically*). But this is my wedding ring. . . .

CHEMIST (*slapping his forehead in anguish*). Wedding rings! You women and your wedding rings! Please don't mention them! For a month I have been trying to persuade my wife to give me hers, so that I could melt it. Vain! I know women! (*He buries his head in his hands and begins to sob.*)

MRS. PETERKIN. Poor man! Here, Agamemnon, give him a drink. (*She hands the cup to* AGAMEMNON *who puts the cup to the mouth of the sobbing* CHEMIST.)

MRS. PETERKIN. Oh! Oh! I forgot! How silly of me!

CHEMIST. What WAS THAT?

AGAMEMNON. Sir, what was that was what we came to you about. This morning my Mother put salt in her coffee instead of sugar and we don't know what to do.

CHEMIST. Well . . . I'm quite busy, as you can see. . . .

MR. PETERKIN. Perhaps we could give you a little gold for your services. . . .

CHEMIST. Gold! Gold! My dear people, what are we waiting for! Must get to work right away! (*rubs hands together*) Hmmmm. (*He dips his finger in coffee and tastes it again. He wrinkles his eyebrows in thought.*) What this needs is a little chlorate of potassium. (*He pours something from a blue bottle and then takes a sip. The* PETERKINS *watch eagerly.*) Not much different, no . . . some bichlorate of magnesia perhaps. . . . (*tries this and tastes again*) On second thought . . . I have it! Some ammonia is just the thing! (*tries it*) No, not the thing at all. (*In rapid succession, he names an acid, pours it, tastes it, rejects it, as the* PETERKINS *each time hold their breath and then release it as a chorus.*) Oxalic acid . . . cyanic acid . . . acetic acid . . . phosphoric acid . . . hyperchloric acid . . . boracic acid . . . silicic acid . . . nitric acid . . . formic acid. . . . Well that's the acids. So much for them!

MR. PETERKIN. With all those bottles you ought to be able to do something!

FIRST LITTLE BOY. Put in some peppermint!

ELIZABETH ELIZA. Shhh! Mother doesn't like peppermint.

AGAMEMNON. I really must try my hand at chemistry. I might have a hidden talent.

SOLOMON JOHN. I really don't see, sir, how you know which is which. You have so many things. It seems very confusing.

(*The* CHEMIST *has been continuing, faster and faster, to put dashes of this and that into the cup and to taste each concoction more and more frantically.*)

CHEMIST. Whew! None of the acids work. Nor calcium . . . barium . . . strontium . . . bitumen . . . belladonna . . . atropine . . . granulated hydrogen . . . potash . . . antimony . . . and a trifle of carbon sprinkled on the top . . . and here . . . try this! (*He tastes a new mixture and smacks his lips.*) Just a third of a fourth of a thirty-secondth of a grain of arsenic! Maybe, maybe! Here!

(*He hands the cup to* AGAMEMNON, *who sips a bit and passes it to* MRS. PETERKIN. *The cup goes down the line and back again. All turn to* MRS. PETERKIN *for her verdict.*)

MRS. PETERKIN. It is a pretty color and it certainly is different, but, well, to be frank with you, it tastes like anything but coffee! (*The others murmur their agreement.*)

CHEMIST. Well, my theory was right even if the experiment has failed. My theory was that all I have put into the coffee should have taken out the salt. The only thing left to do is to try a bit of starch.

MRS. PETERKIN. No, no. No starch, thank you very much.

CHEMIST. Then, my dear people, I should like you to pay me and leave me alone. My gold! Where's my gold? Quick, pay me and you can leave.

(MR. PETERKIN *fishes desperately in his pockets and brings out some coins.*)

MR. PETERKIN. All I have is one dollar and thirty-seven cents in gold.

AGEMEMNON. And gold is now two sixty-nine. That means on the gold market . . . (*He tries to study it out.*)

CHEMIST. Thank you, thank you. Good day to you. Sorry about the coffee. (*He is now down from his stool and he starts to wheel his cart offstage right.* AGAMEMNON *grabs the pencil and pad from the cart, climbs on the stool and starts ciphering. The other* PETERKINS *start to follow the* CHEMIST *and his cart. The* CHEMIST *stops suddenly and turns around; the line of* PETERKINS *almost falls down.*) Where's my pencil? Never mind. I Halbert Stine Stine am about to discover a formula for the most precious, delicious, costly, beautiful . . . (*He is now offstage. The* PETERKINS *stand looking after him.*)

AGAMEMNON. Let's see! $1.37 in gold would be $1.37 times $2.68 . . . carry five . . . why, in heaven's name, did I go to college! (*He stands on the stool, takes down the sign, jumps to the floor and carries stool, sign, pencil and pad off right.*)

MRS. PETERKIN. But what about my coffee?

ALL. Yes, the coffee!

AGAMEMNON (*returning from off right*). Why yes, the coffee!

ELIZABETH ELIZA. Why don't we go to the Herb-Woman?

ALL. (*They jump up and down with joy.*) The Herb-Woman!

MRS. PETERKIN. Elizabeth Eliza, you are right! It was not for nothing we named you after my sister. . . .

MR. PETERKIN. And MY sister!

(*They all troop off happily stage right.*
The HERB-WOMAN *enters from stage left in front of the curtain. She carries a trowel and a little stool. She wears a dark blouse, a full skirt which is covered with pockets in which she has her herbs, and a pointed hat.*)

HERB-WOMAN. Well, it's been a good day's work, even though I did get scratched by the berry bushes. Good sassafras roots (*pats one of her dirty pockets*) and pennyroyal and ever-lasting . . .

(*The* PETERKINS *in line enter from stage right.*)

PETERKINS (*stopping as they see the* HERB-WOMAN). Here she is!

HERB-WOMAN. Yes, here she is! (*She puts down her stool and sits on it.*) But she is tired from digging of a Sunday, and not wishing to meet anyone.

PETERKINS. But, dear Herb-Woman, we have a PROBLEM!

AGAMEMNON. And only you can help us!

LITTLE BOYS. Mother put salt in her coffee . . .

ELIZABETH ELIZA. Sssssh!

LITTLE BOYS. Instead of sugar. . . .

ELIZABETH ELIZA. Sssssh! Agamemnon, you tell!

MRS. PETERKIN. Yes, Agamemnon, you went to college.

HERB-WOMAN. College, follege. What's the matter with you?

AGAMEMNON (*haughtily*). The fact is that Mother put salt in her coffee instead of sugar.

ELIZABETH ELIZA. We went to the Chemist and he made it worse instead of better.

HERB-WOMAN (*disdainfully*). Naturally. You should have come to me.

PETERKINS. Yes, we know.

ELIZABETH ELIZA. And here we are.

MR. PETERKIN. And Mother would very much like to finish her Sunday coffee before Sunday is over.

MRS. PETERKIN. That is certainly true.

MR. PETERKIN. In fact . . .

MRS. PETERKIN. In fact, I am getting quite impatient.

HERB-WOMAN. The Chemist, phah! Hand me the cup! (*The cup is passed to her. She rises, puts the cup on the stool, stands behind the stool and starts rummaging in her pockets.*)

Roley, holey, moley, poley, roley, holey, moley, poley. (*She takes out of her pockets pinches of this and that, adds them to the mixture, stirs with her finger, as she chants.*)

FIRST LITTLE BOY. What's she saying?

SECOND LITTLE BOY. Silly! A magic spell, of course!

THIRD LITTLE BOY. Of course, silly!

HERB-WOMAN. And now we add a little sassafras. Try it! (*She beckons to* MRS. PETERKIN *who comes to the front of the line.*)

MRS. PETERKIN (*tasting*). It tastes like sassafras tea and not at all like coffee.

HERB-WOMAN. (*She pronounces each addition to the mixture and after each, she passes the cup to* MRS. PETERKIN *who tastes and hands the cup back.*) Flagroot . . . snakeroot . . . spruce gum . . . caraway . . . dill . . . rue . . . rosemary . . .

MRS. PETERKIN (*after each taste*). I'm dreadfully sorry, but it does NOT taste like COFFEE.

HERB-WOMAN (*same business of passing and tasting*). Marjoram . . . oppermint . . . sappermint . . . wild thyme . . .

SOLOMON JOHN. Does thyme come from wild clocks?

AGAMEMNON. I'll look it up in the encyclopedia.

HERB-WOMAN. Tansy . . . basil . . . catnip valerian . . . ginger . . . pennyroyal. Toley, poley, holey, moley . . . Squeedunk!

AGEMEMNON. Pardon?

MRS. PETERKIN. Now it tastes worse than ever. Soon I'll be forgetting what real coffee tastes like!

MR. PETERKIN. This certainly will not DO. (*He breaks out of the line and goes to the* HERB-WOMAN.) Here is five cents in currency. For your efforts.

HERB-WOMAN (*tucks the money into a pocket, gets up, takes her stool and starts out left, mumbling to herself*). It's bewitched!

AGAMEMNON. Pardon? I'm sorry, but I didn't quite understand.

HERB-WOMAN (*screaming as she exits*). The Devil Himself's bewitched that coffee!

(*The* PETERKINS *stand in silence.*)

MRS. PETERKIN (*looking at the cup*). Well!

SOLOMON JOHN. It couldn't be all THAT bad!

LITTLE BOYS. She's a witch herself!

ELIZABETH ELIZA. Hush!

MR. PETERKIN. Look what we've done! We've wasted a whole day! And poor Mrs. Peterkin still hasn't got past breakfast!

SOLOMON JOHN. Why not have some tea instead?

ELIZABETH ELIZA. Don't be foolish, Solomon John!

MRS. PETERKIN. It is growing so late. Let's just go home and think.

(*The* PETERKINS *file off sadly, stage left.*

The curtain opens and the PETERKINS *are at home again.* MRS. PETERKIN *is sitting in the chair, holding the cup. The others are in a half circle around her. They are all deep in thought.*)

ELIZABETH ELIZA. If only we knew where the Lady from Philadelphia was. She is so very wise and would know what is best to be done.

(*There is a knock offstage right and the* LADY FROM PHIL-ADELPHIA *enters. She stands and looks at them.*)

PETERKINS. The Lady from Philadelphia! (*The* LITTLE BOYS *run to her and hug her.*)

LADY FROM PHILADELPHIA. Yes . . . Yes . . . It's I. Calm down, everyone. Little Boys, I won't have enough coat to go home in! What's the matter?

(*Everyone begins to talk at once.*)

MR. PETERKIN. Mrs. Peterkin put salt in her coffee instead of sugar and we went to the . . .

AGAMEMNON. Our Mother put salt in her coffee and the Chemist couldn't fix it and the Herb-Woman put time in but . . .

ELIZABETH ELIZA. The poor Chemist was trying to make gold. . . .

SOLOMON JOHN. The Chemist put sulphuric acid in it and it turned blue. . . .

LITTLE BOYS. The Herb-Woman was a witch and she said "moley, moley, bless my souley. . . ."

LADY FROM PHILADELPHIA (*laughing*). Stop! Stop! I can't understand a word you're saying! Who's going to explain it to me?

PETERKINS. Agamemnon!

AGAMEMNON (*embarrassed*). Well . . . uh . . . it's simply this: Mother put salt in her coffee. To put it briefly.

LADY FROM PHILADELPHIA. Well, why doesn't she make a fresh cup of coffee?

(*Everyone is quiet. The amazed family looks from one to another openmouthed.*)

ELIZABETH ELIZA. Why didn't we think of that?

MRS. PETERKIN. Why didn't we think of that?

PETERKINS (*to audience*). Why didn't we think of THAT??

(*curtain*)

PRODUCTION NOTES

The original illustrations and the stories themselves will make you thoroughly acquainted with how each Peterkin looks and acts.

They lived in the nineteenth century in the Victorian period. Mrs. Peterkin, in fact, looks somewhat like a housewifely version of Queen Victoria. She is plump and matronly in her full skirt with its flounced overdrape, and her lace cap.

Elizabeth Eliza is pretty and proper and wears a cameo brooch at the top of her lace-edged, stiff-collared bodice.

The men at this time wore frock coats and tight trousers, with plain or striped or flowered vests. They wore high collars and cravats. They were fond of side whiskers, chin whiskers and mustaches. Mr. Peterkin is very sedately dressed, but Agamemnon and Solomon John like striped suits and gay colors. They all wear big watch chains across their middles. Solomon John, who writes, wears his eyeglasses low on his nose. Mr. Peterkin's glasses are set solidly in their proper place.

The Little Boys wear long pants, short jackets and white blouses with large collars. They are almost always bouncing up and down in their knee-high rubber boots.

The Lady from Philadelphia is fashionable and elegant in a velvet suit, a fur cape, a feathered hat and kid gloves.

Part of the fun of this play is the speed with which it goes. Everything this absurd family does is rather frenzied. It is appropriate that, although they start at home and trudge for miles to the Chemist and then to the Herb-Woman and back home again, the action whirls along. To achieve this speed, the only scene which is set up on the stage itself is the Peterkin parlor, which starts the play and ends it.

The in-between scenes are in front of the curtain and are indicated by props which characters themselves bring on and off. The Chemist wheels his entire laboratory on stage. A tea table on wheels would make a good counter, or a baby carriage which has a board fastened over the top of it. The cart is crowded with bottles and boxes out of which he pretends to pour his liquids and powders. The speed with which he mixes and tastes should be almost dizzying to the audience, as it is to the Peterkins. The Herb-Woman has all of her herbs in her pockets and she carries her own stool.

THE SWINEHERD

THE SWINEHERD

The central theme of this play is from the story by
Hans Christian Andersen.

The stage is an artificial garden. Across the back is a row of
artificial trees cut into very fancy forms. Strange imitation
animals and birds perch in the trees. A few feet in front of the
row of trees is a hedge of artificial bushes, with strange artificial
flowers and butterflies. This hedge is divided at exact up center
to make an entrance to the garden. At stage right and left are
artificial trees which form the sides of the garden. The front
edge of the garden is a low border of artificial flowers. There is a
bit of open space in front of the enclosed garden, where "out-
siders" may walk.

CHARACTERS

THE GARDENER	THE KING
THE GENERAL DOMO	PRINCE TOM
THE PROFESSOR	PRINCESS CELESTRINA
EIGHT ELEGANT LADIES	

*After the audience has had a few moments to look at this
artificial garden,* THE GARDENER *enters from up left. He pushes
a fancy little wheelbarrow. He wears very colorful clothes,
rather like a Pied Piper, and he prances when he walks. He
pushes his barrow into the garden and circles the enclosure,
stopping occasionally to replace a bird, flower or butterfly with a
new one from his barrow. These new ones have large cards
attached to them. When he finishes his tour, he stops up center,
inspects the garden, and nods with satisfaction. Then he turns
to a large cuckoo bird in a bush up center, takes a big key from
his pocket, and winds the bird. Offstage there is a winding
noise. Pushing his wheelbarrow, he exits the way he came.*

THE GENERAL DOMO *enters from up right. He wears military uniform decorated with much braid and many medals. Around his neck is an ornate chain with a splendid watch on it. With very high steps he marches through the garden entrance to down center. He looks at his watch, turns around, and signals to the cuckoo. The cuckoo responds with eight calls.*

Immediately from up left and up right THE LADIES, *in a line of four from each side, enter. The lines meet at the garden entrance and in double line they enter the garden, swaying gracefully, and form a row across the rear of it.* NUMBERS ONE *and* THREE *on each side carry large feather dusters.* NUMBERS TWO *and* FOUR *carry large perfume sprayers. They pose, heads high.*

LADIES (*in very artificial voices*). A delightful morning to you! (*They curtsy deeply and hold the curtsy.*)

GENERAL. More point to the toe! (LADIES *adjust their toes.*) At ease! (LADIES *stand erect.*) More tilt to the nose! More arch to the neck! More lift to the eyebrows! More extension of the little finger! More pucker of the lips!

(THE LADIES *have followed each command.*)

GENERAL. Ah me! You have a regrettable tendency toward naturalness. I trust you will try to curb this fault. Now attention! Present dusters! (THE FOUR LADIES *who carry dusters take one step forward and present their dusters.*) Ready! Dust! (*The four move upstage to the hedge and start dusting the bushes.*) Attention! Present sprayers! (THE FOUR LADIES *who carry perfume sprayers take one step forward and present their sprayers.*) Ready! Perfume! (*These four follow the dusters and spray the flowers with perfume.* THE LADIES, *dusting and spraying, circle the stage until they are back in position across the rear.*) Dismissed!

(THE LADIES *curtsy to* THE GENERAL DOMO *and leave as they entered.* THE GENERAL *signals to the cuckoo and the cuckoo calls nine times. Then* THE GENERAL *marches off.*

THE PROFESSOR *enters from up left and into garden up center. He wears tailcoat and tights, high collar, fancy waistcoat, top hat and ballet slippers. On a chain around his neck is a monocle. He circles the garden critically, eying it through his monocle. The cuckoo calls one very low sound.* THE PROFESSOR *turns and shakes his finger at that impertinent bird.*)

PROFESSOR. That is QUAITE out of order! (*He always speaks in an accent which is fake British garbled with other languages.*)

(THE PROFESSOR *now takes a position up right center.* THE LADIES *re-enter; their props now, instead of dusters and sprayers, are fans which hang on ribbons around their necks. They come through the garden entrance, alternating from left to right. As each one enters, she stands facing* THE PROFESSOR, *puts her left hand on her hip, and extends her right hand droopily to him.* THE PROFESSOR *bows to each* LADY *and kisses her hand.* THE LADIES *then move in a single line and form a semicircle stage right. They pose prettily with their fans open.* THE PROFESSOR *eyes them with his monocle. There is an expectant silence.*)

PRINCESS (*from off up right in thrilling voice*). Hoo-hoo!

(THE PROFESSOR, *as a conductor of an orchestra, waves his hands at* THE LADIES.)

LADIES (*echoing* THE PRINCESS). Hoo-hoo!

(THE PRINCESS *appears at the center opening of the garden, and gives her hand to* THE PROFESSOR. *He greets her with a low bow.*)

PRINCESS. Such a (*she pauses*) . . . *magnifique* morning, Professor!

LADIES (*moving their open fans once*). Magnifique!

PRINCESS. Are there some *magnifique* new gifts today?

LADIES (*moving their fans back*). Magnifique!

PROFESSOR. Shall we tour the garden, Princess?

PRINCESS (*extending her hand to him*). Magnifique!

LADIES. Magnifique!

PROFESSOR (*taking* THE PRINCESS's *hand and holding it high, as in a minuet*). Eet eez my pleasure—quaite! (*He escorts her to the first new gift.*)

PRINCESS (*looking at the card and raising her eyebrows*). What does it say, Professor?

PROFESSOR (*adjusting his monocle and reading*). "Je vous adore. Le Comte d'Alençon."

PRINCESS. Oh, he is . . . ?

PROFESSOR. French.

PRINCESS. French, of course. (*She hesitates.*) Oui! (THE PROFESSOR *nods happily.*)

LADIES (*sweeping their fans*). Oui!

PRINCESS (*at the next gift*). And this?

PROFESSOR (*reading the card*). "Ti voglio bene. Il Principe Geronimo."

PRINCESS. Oh, he is . . . ?

PROFESSOR. Italian.

PRINCESS. Italian, of course. Si! (THE PROFESSOR *nods happily.*)

LADIES (*sweeping their fans*). Si!

PRINCESS (*at the next gift*). And this?

PROFESSOR (*reading that card*). "Ich liebe dich. Der Duke auf Gumultisch."

PRINCESS. And he is . . . ?

PROFESSOR. German.

PRINCESS. German, of course. Ja!

LADIES (*sweeping their fans*). Ja!

PROFESSOR. Eet pleases me QUAITE that you make such progress with ze languages, Princess.

PRINCESS. You are kind, Professor. It is so necessary to be able to language-drop.

PROFESSOR. So. Shall we begin now ze practice of ze language-drop?

PRINCESS. Oui, si, ja.

LADIES (*fanning three times*). Oui, si, ja.

PROFESSOR. Splendide. (*He escorts* THE PRINCESS *to the center of the semicircle of* LADIES *and then takes his own position facing them as conductor.*) First we open ze throat by ze vocalizing. We shall start with ze laughter. Repeat after me. First, ze Hearty Laugh. (*very languidly*) Ho, ho, ho.

LADIES AND PRINCESS. Ho, ho, ho.

PROFESSOR. Ze Scornful laugh. From high to low, pleeze. Ha-ha.

LADIES AND PRINCESS. Ha-ha

PROFESSOR (*nodding*). Gut! Now in ze opposite direction but with ze separation and ze break-off staccato! Zis is for ze laugh of ze chase of courtship. Ze Dodging Laugh. Ha-*ha!*

LADIES AND PRINCESS. Ha-*ha!*

PROFESSOR. Eet must co-ordinate with ze fan. So! (*He uses his hands to demonstrate.*) Ha-*ha!*

LADIES AND PRINCESS. Ha-ha! (*They cover their eyes with their fans.*)

PROFESSOR. And now we try a bit of ze language-dropping. We begin with ze individual repeat. Magnifique!

EACH LADY (*as he points to her*). Magnifique!

PROFESSOR. And togezer! (*He waves both arms.*)

LADIES AND PRINCESS. Magnifique!

PROFESSOR. And today we add Superbe. First in ze chorus only. Superbe!

LADIES AND PRINCESS. Superbe!

PROFESSOR. Charmant!

LADIES AND PRINCESS. Charmant!

PROFESSOR. Eet is gut to have zeeze words from ze French. But to be QUAITE accomplished you should have also ze same in Italian and in ze German. Ze German: wunderbar, voooonderbarrrr!

LADIES AND PRINCESS (*with some difficulty*). Voooooderbarrrr!

PROFESSOR. And ze Italian—meraviglioso. Mer-a-vig-li-oso!

LADIES AND PRINCESS. Mer-a-vig-li-oso!

PROFESSOR. Zeeze are all ze words you need except for ze Yes.

LADIES AND PRINCESS (*quickly*). Oui, si, ja.

PROFESSOR. . . . and ze No.

LADIES AND PRINCESS. Non, No, Nein.

PROFESSOR. But wiz ze No eet is better ze question. Non? No? Nein?

LADIES AND PRINCESS. Non? No? Nein?

PROFESSOR. And ze most useful word of all: ze Why. Pourquoi? Perchè? Warrrroooom? Wiz ze fans, Please.

LADIES AND PRINCESS (*with fans at eyes, flirtatiously*). Pour-quoi? Perchè? Warrrrrooooom?

PROFESSOR. And now we practice ze language-drop in song. Eet is very important to know ze line or two of ze song. Eet come in handy in many unexpected situations. Ze first, ze "Alouette."

LADIES AND PRINCESS (*singing as he conducts*). "Alouette, gentille alouette, Alouette, je te plumerai." (*They stop abruptly.*)

PROFESSOR. You must learn to end with ze trail-off to mean you know more. Again, now, with ze trail-off. (*He demonstrates.* "te plum-er-ai . . ."

LADIES AND PRINCESS (*sing*). "Alouette, gentille alouette, Alouette, je te plum-er-ai. . . ." (They end with a little hum.)

PROFESSOR. Now with ze same trail-off with "Santa Lucia."

LADIES AND PRINCESS (*as he conducts*). "Sul Marie Luccioca L'astro d'argento. . . ." (*They trail off into a hum.*)

PROFESSOR. And now with ze "Ach du Lieber Augustin."

LADIES AND PRINCESS. "Ach du lieber Augustin, Alles ist weg, weg, weg. . . ."

PROFESSOR. Superbe! Meraviglioso! Wunderbar! (*He applauds high in the air gracefully.*) So, we must not overdo. We must now rest. Play ze quiet games now. So, Ladies, Princess, until tomorrow! (*He bows deeply and exits up left.*)

(THE LADIES *bow to him as he leaves. Now they stand drooping.*)

PRINCESS. How shall we amuse ourselves? I am weary of all the quiet games! (*She walks about the garden and looks again at her new presents.*)

FIRST LADY. Shall we wind up the birds and have them sing to us?

(THE LADIES *flit around the garden and stand in front of the birds.*)

PRINCESS. I tire of that game. My suitors have so little imagination. Can they find nothing original? (THE LADIES *droop.*)

SECOND LADY. Shall we play Court Gossip?

(THE LADIES *run to make a little circle stage right, heads together and arms around each other.*)

PRINCESS. Is there anything new at court to gossip about?

(THE LADIES *shrug and turn around in their circle, drooping.*)

KING (*appearing up center*). My dear Daughter and Ladies! (THE LADIES *bow deeply.*)

PRINCESS. PaPA! Have you a new toy for us? We weary of the ones we have.

KING. My dear Celestrina, your Papa does the best he can. Yes, he has brought you a new toy. Another suitor has come. A Prince with new gifts.

PRINCESS. Better than the ones I have, I hope. What are they?

KING. He insists on giving them to you himself.

PRINCESS. That is an amusing idea. Have him enter! Perhaps he will divert us.

KING. Take your poses, then, for the Receiving of a Suitor.

(THE LADIES *pose in a semicircle stage left.* THE PRINCESS *takes her place in front of them. All open their fans.*)

KING. And don't forget your language-dropping. I pay the Professor a pretty penny to educate you! (*He stands stage right.*)

(PRINCE TOM *appears with* THE GENERAL DOMO *behind him.* THE GENERAL *carries a tray on which is a beautiful box.* THE GENERAL *stands in the entrance up center, as* PRINCE TOM *enters the garden.*)

GENERAL. Prince Tom!

(THE PRINCE *goes immediately to* THE PRINCESS *and bows to her.* THE PRINCESS *extends her hand high in the air.*)

PRINCE (*looks at the hand in surprise, takes it down and kisses it*). Dear Princess, I am honored. I have heard of your beauty and have longed to see you.

PRINCESS (*coyly*). Oui?

PRINCE (*emphatically*). Yes!

PRINCESS. Do you come from a great kingdom, Prince Tom?

PRINCE. No, it is only a tiny kingdom, but a beautiful one.

PRINCESS. A tiny kingdom?

PRINCE. Yes, it is small. But it is in the high mountains and it is full of flowers and birds and devoted subjects who farm the upland valleys and have high holidays in the hills.

PRINCESS. How quaint! (*She turns to her* LADIES *and laughs the scornful laugh, curved from high to low.*) Haaaaaa!

LADIES (*echoing*). Haaaaaa!

PRINCESS. What nice new toys have you brought me?

PRINCE (*puzzled*). Toys? No toys. I have brought you the most beautiful thing I could find.

PRINCESS. Is it truly magnifique?

LADIES (*echoing*). Magnifique?

PRINCE (*simply*). I hope you will like it. (*He turns to* THE GENERAL DOMO, *takes the box from the tray, and holds it toward* THE PRINCESS. THE LADIES *close in on tiptoe to look.* THE KING *steps up to look over* THE PRINCE's *shoulder.* THE GENERAL *comes beside* THE KING *to peer.*)

PRINCESS (*opening the box, which* THE PRINCE *holds, and looking inside*). Oh, superbe!

LADIES (*looking*). Superbe!

PRINCESS. Where did you find it? I have never seen anything like it!

PRINCE. In a very special place in the high hills.

PRINCESS. How exquisitely it is made! What does it do?

PRINCE. Do?

PRINCESS. What are its magic tricks?

PRINCE. Magic tricks? Well . . . for me it does magic. Smell it and see if it does magic tricks for you.

PRINCESS (*takes out of the box a white rose and smells it*). The odor is very faint.

LADIES (*sniffing*). Very faint!

PRINCESS. We will spray it with perfume.

PRINCE. Spray it with perfume?

PRINCESS. Of course . . . after we have put it in position in the garden.

PRINCE. But it will last only a few more moments. I wrapped its stem in moss to keep it until you could see it. Its beauty and its perfume are only for you and only for now!

PRINCESS. Then how can it be my toy?

PRINCE. It is not a toy, Princess. It is a real rose.

LADIES, KING, GENERAL, PRINCESS (*horrified*). REAL?

PRINCESS. Oh fie, Papa! He has fooled me! It is not artificial!

KING (*sadly*). It is so well made I would not think it could be real.

PRINCESS. Papa, we have been insulted! (*She throws the rose to the ground.*)

PRINCE (*picking up the rose*). Yes, it is a real rose. But I have not given it to a real Princess. (*He bows curtly, and jumps over the front flower border and runs off downstage left.*)

PRINCESS. PAPA!!

KING AND GENERAL (*rushing down to front border*). SCOUN-
DREL!!

PRINCESS AND LADIES (*rushing to either side of* KING *and*
GENERAL). Scoundrel!!

KING (*drawing himself up*). Princess and Ladies! We are all
behaving in a most ridiculous fashion. Let us say merely that
it was a moment of diversion and let us forget the whole
stupid affair. I shall order the guards at the border of my
kingdom to keep a tighter watch for intruders.

GENERAL (*looking at the tray, where* THE PRINCE *has replaced
the box*). And this?

PRINCESS. I shall use it for a trinket box.

KING. That is a proper use for it!

(*The cuckoo calls ten times.* THE GENERAL *whirls around
and looks at the bird.* THE LADIES *and* THE PRINCESS *are
still looking off downstage left.*)

GENERAL. LADIES! The Mistress of the Wardrobe is waiting
for you. (*He walks upstage center and turns back.*)
LADIES!! (*He claps his hands impatiently.*) LADIES!!
(THE LADIES *turn to him, but* THE PRINCESS *is still looking
offstage.*) Positions, Please! (THE LADIES *straighten their
backs.*) More tilt to the nose, IF you please. (*Their heads go
high.*)

KING. My dear daughter, Celestrina, have you forgotten your
training?

PRINCESS. Non, Papa! (*She turns and joins the line of* LADIES.)

GENERAL. Princess and Ladies! It is at just such a time that the
song is helpful. (*He leads them off as they sing the first lines
of the three songs they have practiced.*)

KING. (*Alone now on stage, he walks around sadly, looking at
the artificial birds and flowers. At the upstage exit of the*

• 35 •

garden, he stops and sighs.) Being a King and a Father is difficult!

(*The cuckoo sounds one call very softly, as if in answer to* THE KING.)

GARDENER (*entering from up left*). Your Highness.

KING. How did you know I wanted to see you?

GARDENER. I didn't know, Your Highness; I just came to tell you . . .

KING. Well I do want to see you. There is something the matter with that cuckoo.

GARDENER. Yes, Your Highness?

KING. See that it is replaced with a reliable one.

GARDENER. Yes, Your Highness. I will go back for my tools. I came to tell you that there is a person asking for a position in your service, Your Highness.

KING. What kind of person?

GARDENER. A lowly person, sir. We do need a new swineherd, Your Highness, as I have been telling you.

KING (*sniffing*). If we need a new swineherd, that is your affair; not mine. (*He strides off up right.*)

GARDENER (*looking at cuckoo*). I'll get my tools and remove you and then you'll be sorry!

(*The lowly person, in ragged clothing with a cap worn low on his forehead and a face that is dirt-smeared, has entered the garden. It is* THE PRINCE *in disguise. He carries a little pot, which has on its rim bells that tinkle.*)

GARDENER (*turning and seeing the person*). Oh! Oh! You should *not* have come into the garden! I told you to wait!

PRINCE. What did the King say? May I be in his service?

· ·

GARDENER. You can! You can be (*laughs*)—the Imperial Swineherd. Follow me with your cooking pot and I'll show you the shed near the pigsties where you will live. (*He prances to downstage and steps over the front flower border, followed by* THE PRINCE.)

(*At this moment* THE PRINCESS *enters up center, singing woefully "Ach du Lieber Augustin." Her* LADIES *follow her in a single line. She comes center and* THE LADIES *form a semicircle behind her. They all have sung the only two lines they know of the song.* THE GARDENER *has stopped at the downstage right exit; so has* THE PRINCE. *The little pot is playing the same tune, and when* THE LADIES *stop singing the pot goes on merrily playing the rest of the song.*)

PRINCESS. That is our tune! Gardener! Who is that person who has our tune?

GARDENER. My Lady, he is the new Swineherd and I am showing him the way to the pigsties!

PRINCESS. I wish him to remain here for a moment. He will follow you later. You may go, Gardener.

GARDENER (*in surprise*). Yes, Your Highness. (*He prances off.*)

PRINCESS (*turns to* FIRST LADY *and whispers to her*). Go on! (*shoves her*)

FIRST LADY (*advancing haughtily toward* THE PRINCE). The Princess would like to have that musical instrument.

PRINCE. Sorry! It is my cooking pot. It plays tunes to keep me happy, and, when I cook in it, the steam from it makes me smell all the dinners that are being cooked on every stove in the countryside. So I can enjoy all kinds of good food in my imagination, when I cook my own simple food.

(*The pot keeps playing, as* FIRST LADY *runs back and whispers to* THE PRINCESS. THE PRINCESS *whispers to* THE SECOND LADY. *All the others listen.*)

SECOND LADY (*coming down to* PRINCE). The Princess will pay you any price you ask for the pot.

PRINCE. Then you may tell her . . . (*He whispers to* SECOND LADY.)

SECOND LADY. Non, no, nein!!

PRINCE. I won't take less!

SECOND LADY (*running back to the group*). Princess! Princess!

PRINCESS. Well, what does he say?

SECOND LADY. I really cannot tell you! It is too shocking! He says . . . he says . . . he must have twenty kisses from the Princess!

PRINCESS. He is a wretch! (*The pot is now playing "Alouette."* THE PRINCESS *listens, and then whispers to* THE THIRD LADY.)

THIRD LADY (*coming down to* PRINCE). The Princess says will you take the twenty kisses from the Ladies instead?

PRINCE (*loudly*). No, thank you! Twenty kisses from the Princess, or I keep my pot! (THIRD LADY *returns to group.*)

PRINCESS. How tiresome he is. Listen to the pot! Now it is playing "Santa Lucia." It knows ALL of our tunes. And if we had the pot, we could tell what everyone is having for dinner. What an amusing bit of gossip that would be!

LADIES. How amusing!

PRINCESS. I have never heard finer music.

LADIES (*eagerly*). Never!

PRINCESS. And one should encourage art!

LADIES. Oui, si, ja!

(THE PRINCESS *whispers to* FOURTH LADY.)

FOURTH LADY (*going to* THE PRINCE). You may bring the pot. (*She goes back to the group.*)

PRINCE (*steps over the flower border and goes to* THE PRINCESS, *who reaches out for the pot. He puts it behind him*). The payment first, please.

PRINCESS. The Ladies will all have to stand around me, so that no passerby can see.

LADIES (*making a circle around* THE PRINCESS *and* THE PRINCE, *and spreading out their skirts. They start counting*). One . . . Ah! Two . . . Ah! Three . . .

(*The counting continues, as* THE GARDENER *returns down right with his tools. He is followed by* THE KING.)

KING. Where is he?

GARDENER. I left him here, Your Highness. The Princess told me to go.

KING. This is MOST irregular of the Princess! You were right to come tell me! But where is he? And what is this game the Ladies are playing?

(THE KING *tiptoes up to look. He peers over the backs of* THE LADIES, *who keep on with the counting.*)

LADIES. Twenty!!

KING (*bellowing*). WHAT IS THIS???

(THE LADIES *whirl around and see* THE KING. *They run in terror behind* THE PRINCESS. *She has the pot in her arms.* THE PRINCE *is laughing.*)

KING. MY DAUGHTER KISSING A SWINEHERD!! This is the most disgraceful thing that has ever happened in all of my days of being King and Father!

PRINCESS. Nonsense, Papa! I only wanted this magic toy!

KING. For a magic toy you have degraded yourself by kissing a Swineherd. When you have scorned suitor after suitor! I hereby DISOWN you! Go with your Swineherd out of my kingdom forever!

PRINCESS. But Papa, I just wanted a new toy! Surely you don't mean that I am to go away with a Swineherd! I will accept any one of my suitors, even that last silly one who brought nothing but a real rose.

PRINCE (*taking the rose out of his pocket*). Even that one? I AM that Prince!

EVERYONE. YOU???

KING (*happily*). Then take off that stupid disguise and BE the Prince you are. Now that you have kissed my daughter, you may marry her and we will say all's well that ends well.

PRINCESS. Yes, Papa. That is so much better than being cast off with a Swineherd!

PRINCE. I despise you, Princess Celestrina! I came back to despise you! You would not have me as an honorable Prince. You threw away my beautiful rose! But you would kiss a Swineherd for a silly musical toy! Stay here in your artificial kingdom! I'm off to a REAL one! (*He leaps over the front border and runs off singing.*)

(THE KING, THE LADIES, THE PRINCESS *look after the departing* PRINCE. *The pot, which* THE PRINCESS *is holding, starts playing "Ach du Lieber Augustin." The cuckoo calls impertinently.* THE GARDENER *starts toward it with his tools, as the curtain closes.*)

PRODUCTION NOTES

Most storybook princesses are good as well as beautiful. Or if they are not good at the beginning, they become good by the end of the story, so that they may live happily ever after.

Hans Christian Andersen wrote a fairy tale about a princess who was spoiled, stupid, conceited and bored. This play is about her and about the kingdom in which she lived, where only artificial things were considered worth while. The Princess meets a Prince who will never be bored because he knows what is really worth while. When the Prince realizes what the Princess is like, he scorns her and her kingdom. If you think this is too unhappy an ending, you can change it. Perhaps you prefer to have the Princess learn her lesson and run after the Prince to join him in his own simple, natural, delightful life. This might be better. You decide.

Since this is the Kingdom of Artificiality, everything in it is stiff and lifeless. All of the scenery and props in the garden are exaggerated in size, color and pattern. You can have fun designing fantastic birds, butterflies, trees, flowers. They are not beautiful; they are gaudy and harsh. That is why the white rose is so out of place.

The characters in this garden are as artificial as the props. Their dress is formal and overelaborate. Their speech, gestures and movements are stiff and unnatural, patterned from practice.

There are only a few tricks to work out in this play. The noise of winding up the cuckoo and the cuckoo calls can easily be done by an actor behind the cuckoo's hedge. The tunes of the musical pot are very easy ones; an offstage musician could play them on a xylophone. The actors by their pantomime must make the audience believe that the music comes from the pot itself.

If you do this play outdoors, use the same scenery that you would use indoors. To have an artificial garden set in the midst of real outdoor beauty would be very effective and would show even more clearly how stupid this kingdom is. Have the Prince refer by words and gestures to the real world of sky, grass, trees, hills, flowers, birds. Have him climb a real hill at the end of the play while all the left-behinds look after him into a real world.

THE MINIATURE DARZIS

THE MINIATURE DARZIS

(With thanks to Nancy Braxton, Anna Alexander,
Jean Hinson and Gajinder Singh, who helped
make the details accurate)

Lisa Gregg adapted the familiar Grimm's story, "The Elves and
the Shoemaker," and transplanted it to India. She wrote this
play when she was fourteen years old, after spending four years
with her family in India.

The play takes place in Muttra, a small town in Northern
India. The main character is a darzi, an Indian tailor, named
Gokul. His shop, which is the scene of the play, is in a typical
Indian bazaar, a market place, where all kinds of small open-
front shops crowd together with merchandise overflowing into
the street.

Customers remove their sandals at the entrance to the shop.
When one character greets another and when he departs, he
puts his hands together, palm against palm, and says "Namaste." This word is also the name of the action, which is called
"namaste-ing." "Namaste-ji" is a more respectful greeting.

This is how the Indian words in the play are pronounced:

> darzi: *DER-zee*
> namaste: *nah-muh-STAY*
> ji: *gee*
> sahib: *sob*
> salivar cumuz: *SAL-war kaMEEZ*
> chunee: *CHOO-nee*
> choli: *CHO-lee*
> sari: *sorry*
> achkan: *AHTCH-kahn*

GOKUL, A DARZI, ABOUT SEVENTY YEARS OLD

HIS CUSTOMERS: ELVES:

CHANDRAGUPTA SAHIB   RAM

MISS KAPUR   LAL

MRS. SINGH   MOHAN

The scene is the single room of GOKUL's *shop. The two side
walls of the shop are screens painted to look like shelves filled
with rolls of brightly colored cloth. The back wall has real
shelves with real bolts of cloth on them. The bolts of cloth are
arranged so the ends of the rolls are toward the audience. There
are also shelves for hangers, ribbons (which are hanging out),
and boxes for decorations like sequins, beads, braid, brocade,
etc. One shelf has* GOKUL's *notebooks, and copies of* Femina (*a
woman's magazine*) *on it. Scissors, measuring tape, thread and
other tailor's equipment hang from nails. Paper patterns of
costumes may also hang from the walls.*

*Platforms covered with white sheets are against all three sides
of the shop, leaving an empty area in the center that is covered
with mats. The* DARZI *usually sits, cross-legged, on the platform
at stage right where there is a small hand sewing machine. His
customers sit on the opposite platform, or stand in the center
area. The platforms serve as places to sit, stand, display material
or write notes, according to the need. At the top of the stage is a
sign reading "Best Darzi in Whole India." Several steps lead
from the center aisle of the audience to the stage.*

The play begins with bazaar music. GOKUL *enters from stage
right and opens the curtain, as if he were opening his shop for
the day. He is busy arranging his shop, and is standing on
tiptoe on the rear platform straightening cloth on the top shelf,
as* CHANDRAGUPTA SAHIB *comes down the center aisle of the
audience, mounts the steps of the shop, and removes his shoes.
The music fades out.*

GOKUL (*turns while still on tiptoe, and namastes*). Namaste-ji,
Chandragupta Sahib. You are coming to buy some cloth,

isn't it? I am just having new silk from Benares. I have the best silks in all Muttra.

CHANDRAGUPTA (*namastes and peers at shelves*). New stock, eh? Interesting. I would like you to make me one achkan.

GOKUL (*rubbing his hands with pleasure*). Of course, of course, Chandragupta Sahib. May I be pleased to show you . . .

CHANDRAGUPTA. And I must have this achkan cleaned and pressed by tomorrow.

GOKUL (*raising his hands in surprise*). But, sahib, in a single day! How can I make one achkan in a day and clean it too? It is indeed impossible. To make it I will be needing at least three days.

CHANDRAGUPTA (*shrugs and goes back down one step*). Then I will find a new darzi.

GOKUL (*jumps down from platform and rushes to* CHANDRA-GUPTA). Oh no, no, no! I am the best darzi in Muttra. It is disgrace to go to another darzi. I will make it for you. For am I not the best darzi in whole India?

CHANDRAGUPTA (*steps up again*). Humph! I doubt it. But you are a good darzi. (*sits cross-legged on platform stage left*)

GOKUL (*sits stage right*). Now, now, you want what kind of achkan? I have wonderful wool, whole way from England. Or you want something more sportier? This fine raw silk, for example. (*goes to rear platform and pulls a bolt of cloth from shelf*)

CHANDRAGUPTA. I wish gray wool, thank you. It must be good and strong and not show wrinkles.

GOKUL (*reaches for another bolt*). Here is exactly the cloth you want. (*brings it to* CHANDRAGUPTA) Feel the texture, very strong, exactly the right thing for travel. You like?

CHANDRAGUPTA (*fingering it*). Hmmmmm . . . all right. It is not bad cloth.

GOKUL. Fine! I have your measurements. (*gets notebook from shelf*) Here they are. You have very good taste. That is most excellent material. It will be costing you rupees fifty only.

CHANDRAGUPTA. Ah, no, then. (*gets up to leave*) My brother's darzi can make it for much less. (*starts toward steps*)

GOKUL (*moves quickly in front of* CHANDRAGUPTA *to block his way*). But, sahib, what other darzi can make a fine achkan in a single day?

CHANDRAGUPTA. I pay no more than rupees forty to any darzi for any achkan.

GOKUL. You give me more time, the cost will be rupees forty-five only. (CHANDRAGUPTA *starts to go around* GOKUL.) You are sure you are needing it tomorrow?

CHANDRAGUPTA. I am quite sure.

GOKUL (*sees* MISS KAPUR *coming down center aisle*). For rupees forty-two I will make it.

CHANDRAGUPTA (*hurriedly, as* MISS KAPUR *starts up steps*). That will be fine. Ah! Namaste, Miss Kapur! (*gestures*)

(CHANDRAGUPTA *and* GOKUL, *who have been blocking steps, part to allow* MISS KAPUR *to enter.* CHANDRAGUPTA *steps down and* GOKUL *steps up.*)

MISS KAPUR. (*She is young, but is trying to act grown-up.*) Ah, Chandragupta Sahib. Namaste. (*gestures*) Beautiful day, isn't it?

CHANDRAGUPTA. Wonderful day. You are looking sweet today. So nice seeing you, Miss Kapur. Namaste! (*gestures and exits*)

MISS KAPUR. Namaste! (*She namastes first to* CHANDRAGUPTA *as he departs and then to* GOKUL, *who returns her greeting.*) Ah, you are not busy; I am very glad. (*She sits on left platform and arranges herself gracefully.*) You must make me a salivar cumuz and a chunee. I have an invitation to

Maharajah's tea and I need a new salivar cumuz due to this reason.

GOKUL (*bowing*). You are coming, most certainly, to the finest darzi in Muttra, or in whole India to be sure. (*sits platform right*)

MISS KAPUR. Oh, I know this. This is why I am coming to you. And I need it for tomorrow and Mother was telling me you are the quickest darzi in Muttra.

GOKUL. Well, I am very busy. But for the beautiful young lady, I will make anything.

MISS KAPUR (*giggling*). Oh, you are teasing me. (*pats her hair*)

GOKUL. You have some idea for your salivar cumuz?

MISS KAPUR. No. Mother said you must show me the latest styles from Delhi.

GOKUL. Of course, of course. (*stands*) Here is the latest magazine with pictures of new styles. (*gets large* Femina *magazine from shelf, turns to her and displays it, then puts it on platform next to her*)

MISS KAPUR (*turning pages eagerly*). Oh, look at that! How beautiful this is! Oh, I want this one very much, but will Mother like it?

GOKUL. I do not know, Miss. Perhaps not?

MISS KAPUR. Better to take this one. I am sure she will like this one.

GOKUL. Which one, Miss?

MISS KAPUR. This one. With little beads over the whole thing.

GOKUL. I am thinking your mother would like one with not so many little beads. . . .

MISS KAPUR (*frowning*). You are a silly darzi. This salivar cumuz is not for Mother. It is for me.

GOKUL. Certainly, Miss, but . . .

MISS KAPUR (*makes gesture as if to leave*). If you cannot make the salivar cumuz with little beads, I know another darzi. . . .

GOKUL. I am the only darzi for making such a salivar cumuz. You must remember. This is why you come to me.

MISS KAPUR (*stands*). You must begin immediately. Hurry! Use measurements from the other one you made me. (*starts to leave*)

GOKUL. About the price, Miss. . . .

MISS KAPUR. I know nothing about that. You will discuss that with Mother. Namaste! (*gestures*)

GOKUL. Very well. Tomorrow you will have a beautiful salivar. Namaste, Miss Kapur. (*gestures*)

(MISS KAPUR *turns to leave and almost knocks down* MRS. SINGH, *who is just starting up the stairs from the aisle.*)

MRS. SINGH. Please, Miss Kapur. Must you be rushing in such a manner?

MISS KAPUR. Oh, very sorry, Mrs. Singh. But I am in so much hurry and so excited. Tea at Maharajah's! And little beads over the whole thing. (*runs down steps and off*)

MRS. SINGH. Such manners in young people nowadays!

GOKUL. Namaste-ji. (*gestures*) It is a great pleasure that you are coming to my shop. It is not often enough that I see you. How are your children? (*He gestures for her to sit down; she ignores him.*)

MRS. SINGH. Namaste, Gokul. The children are well. Indeed, that is why I am coming to see you. You are such an expert on making all clothings. I know you are the darzi I need.

GOKUL. I, Gokul, can make anything. Anything.

MRS. SINGH. Please, Gokul. I have no time to waste. And I am thinking you have none also.

GOKUL. Yes, Mrs. Singh. I am a very busy man, and so, important man also, isn't it?

MRS. SINGH. Don't brag with me. It is a waste of time to be coming here, when you are puffed up like a balloon. Really. I cannot understand how you can make a living, when you waste so much time boasting.

GOKUL. Mrs. Singh, you are doing me an injustice!

MRS. SINGH. I am a good customer, and you take all customers you can get. But never mind. I have more important business. My daughter will be married in the next fortnight.

GOKUL. May I be the first sincere darzi to wish her congratulations. (*bows*) Who is the most fortunate man?

MRS. SINGH. Gaatam Kangilal.

GOKUL. A good match. Such a fine couple they will make.

MRS. SINGH. We will go to Benares for the marriage. The whole family. So her wedding outfit must be ready tomorrow. Mine must be ready too, and sahib's also.

GOKUL (*shocked*). Three! Oh, how can I do that in a single night?

MRS. SINGH. You yourself said you were a good darzi.

GOKUL. But THREE?

MRS. SINGH. Yes, three! Manju's will be very simple. Only take six yards of that red silk (*pointing to a bolt on the shelf*). I hope it is the best?

GOKUL (*gets it from shelf*). Of course, of course! I have only the best silks. But still, Mrs. Singh, I am a good darzi but even the best darzi cannot do that!

MRS. SINGH. Please, Gokul, you annoy me! I want you to take that red and gold brocade . . . (GOKUL *reaches for brocade and notebook and tries to write and demonstrate at the same time.*) . . . and sew it to one end of the sari and also around the bottom part. You understand? Then I want you to embroider the edges very carefully. Finally, the choli must be of the same brocade.

GOKUL (*desperately writing*). Yes, yes, yes. Which embroidery?

MRS. SINGH. Well, I guess you can make simple elephants. Make them in gold, of course. Now. Where are your ready-made saris?

GOKUL (*placing a pile of saris from the shelf on platform beside her*). These are saris most suitable for celebrations.

MRS. SINGH (*fingering a green sari*). This green sari is very excellent for me. It is Benares silk? Hm, must be! I'll have it. Make me a matching choli. Embroider a simple design in green on it. The sahib's is regular white. . . .

GOKUL (*writing*). Regular white . . .

MRS. SINGH. . . . But very sleek and elegant. Of course you have our measurements.

GOKUL. Of course. A good darzi always has his best customers' measurements.

MRS. SINGH. Very well. I will be coming for them tomorrow morning. Namaste. (*exits*)

GOKUL. But the price? (*shrugs*) Namaste-ji. (*He makes a halfhearted gesture as he watches* MRS. SINGH *go. Then he turns and surveys his shop, strewn with materials, notes and drawings.*) Ah, ah, ah! A long night's work! An impossible night's work! Before I start, I must go to the temple and pray. That is far more important than all the clothes in the whole world.

(GOKUL *walks down steps and exits up center aisle of audience. Lights dim to denote passing of time, and bazaar music plays softly in background. As* GOKUL *returns, music fades. He comes back into his shop and walks around it, picking up one piece of material after another as he talks.*)

GOKUL. Now let me see, how I shall start? It is now six o'clock. Sahib's achkan he must have tomorrow. (*picks up gray cloth and looks at his notes*) Oh no! Better to start with Miss Kapur's salivar cumuz. (*looks at magazine picture*) So many beads! But then . . . Mrs. Singh's clothes. (*looks at notebook*) Oh, oh, oh. (*hands on head*) With so much work I can never finish. Even working the whole night, I can never finish. I am thinking I am not the best darzi in whole India. The best darzi never would allow himself so many troubles. Why was I saying I can do it? Why am I boasting so much? Why is each one needing his clothes tomorrow? If they are not ready, they will be very angry and I will lose customers. But five! Impossible; It is more than six o'clock and the clothes are not yet cut. I will make sahib's first. Measurements . . . hm! 36, 30, 48, 47 . . . I need some more help. . . .

(*The lights dim on* GOKUL *as he starts to cut the cloth. As a gong strikes twelve times, the lights come up again on* GOKUL, *sitting on the platform at right, drowsily sewing.*)

GOKUL. Twelve o'clock and still there is so much to do. And I am so sleepy . . . so sleepy . . . must not sleep. . . . (*He nods, lowers his head slowly and rests it on sewing machine.*) Zzzzzzzzz!

(*As* GOKUL *falls asleep and begins snoring, soft music and laughter are heard.* RAM *pokes his head out from stage left, sneaks up to* GOKUL *and twitches his clothes. Then he waves and* LAL *and* MOHAN *appear from stage right.*)

RAM. Shh! Be quiet and come here.

(*The other two come up to look at sleeping* GOKUL.)

LAL. Poor Gokul! So silly he is! He brags and brags.

RAM. Shhh! (GOKUL *stirs in sleep.*)

LAL. But he is a good man and goes to the temple every day for praying. We are going to do what thing?

RAM. Assist him, of course. So foolish he is. He is boasting all the time, but he is a good man. He prays every day and he is a kind and considerate man, helping people all the time. Today he went too far in order to please others.

MOHAN. How can we help him?

LAL. We will help him to stay awake! (*Starts to push* GOKUL)

RAM (*stopping him*). Indeed! No! We are going to make clothes for him. With our magical powers.

MOHAN. We have magical powers?

LAL (*scaring little* MOHAN). Boo! I could change you into a stone, if I wanted to.

RAM. Don't tease Mohan, Lal. Mohan, Lal, we must plan. Come now.

MOHAN. I can cut cloth very straight and true. That's me!

RAM. Shh! Don't wake Gokul. He is very tired due to boasting all day. You cut the cloth, Mohan. Be careful you do not drop anything. Let's see. It is blue cloth, red cloth and white cloth we need. Lal, you take the cloth while I get Gokul's notes and measurements.

LAL. The cloth is already here. What shall I do? I am a very good sewer.

RAM. If you can sew and Mohan can cut and I can embroider, then we can do it.

MOHAN. Which one first? Please, let us do the blue salivar cumuz?

LAL. Let us finish the achkan. It is almost done.

RAM. You, Mohan, cut the blue salivar cumuz and you, Lal, finish sewing the achkan. I will draw measurements of the other clothes and then begin the embroidery.

(LAL *starts to lift* GOKUL's *head from sewing machine.*)

RAM (*grabs him*). What you are doing? Leave him sleeping.

LAL. But if I am to sew the achkan . . .

RAM. What are your magical powers for? The sewing machine makes too much noise and is not so good a sewer as you.

(LAL *sits upstage of* GOKUL *and sews achkan with imaginary needle and thread.* MOHAN, *on platform center rear, cuts blue material with imaginary scissors.* RAM, *on platform stage left, measures other material. Soft music plays to suggest passage of time.*)

RAM. Mohan, take these cholis and iron them. But sure you do it well. I will begin embroidering elephants on the marriage sari.

MOHAN. Why do you not iron them yourself?

RAM. I am busy. Shh!

(MOHAN, *using imaginary iron, presses cholis on center platform.* RAM *and* LAL *sew.* LAL *is mumbling to himself.*)

RAM. What you are muttering?

LAL. Some verses.

RAM. Verses! Why are you muttering poetry? You do not have some better thing to be thinking about?

LAL. There is no better thing to think about. And I am learning to be a poet. How do you like this one?

As long as the moon is playing with the gulls . . .
I know I can never be dull.

MOHAN (*laughs*). Fine poet you are!

LAL. You cannot understand verses. You are only jealous because I have much talent.

(GOKUL *almost awakens.*)

RAM. Shh! Quick, hide! (*They duck underneath the material they are working with.* GOKUL *snores. Cautiously they emerge.*) See, Lal, your verses disturb even Gokul!

LAL. Be silent! Let us work. We must hurry if we are really to help Gokul.

(*Soft music plays and lights grow dim while all three work happily. Bits of cloth are tossed out occasionally. Lights come up again and most of the material has disappeared; finished costumes are hanging on hangers from nails in the shelves.*)

MOHAN. Soon we will be finished, and it's only five o'clock. They are beautiful, aren't they? Such excellence! Gokul could not do better, even if he is the best darzi in whole India!

LAL (*to* MOHAN). Hang up this achkan.

(MOHAN *takes hanger from shelf, places achkan on it, and hangs it from nail.*)

RAM. All is finished. Now Gokul can wake up and think he did this work. Better we should leave; sunrise is coming, and light can awaken him. We have done our work. Let us hope Gokul has learned his lesson and will not be needing our help again.

(*With their fingers on their lips, the three do a soft little dance around the shop and then disappear left. There is laughter from offstage. Lights come up, as* GOKUL *wakens.*)

GOKUL (*rubbing his eyes and yawning*). Strange. I am thinking I heard somebody. Music? Laughter? No, no! I must have fallen asleep. (*sees the costumes*) No! But how is it all the clothes are finished? Can I do such a thing in my sleep? (*He walks around the shop and looks at the clothes. He looks carefully at red sari.*) It is most strange. But it is the most delicate and beautiful work that ever I saw. Someone did it for me. Such fine embroidery. Such small stitches with every

· 56 ·

thread in place. Such craftsmanship. Must be magic work. No human could do such magnificent sewing.

(*As bazaar music plays,* CHANDRAGUPTA SAHIB *comes down aisle and mounts steps to shop.*)

CHANDRAGUPTA. Namaste, Gokul. (*gestures*) You are looking well this morning. I hope my achkan is ready.

GOKUL. Namaste-ji. (*gestures*) It is a great pleasure to see you this morning. A fine clear morning. Yes, yes. (*gets achkan on hanger*) And here is your achkan!

CHANRAGUPTA (*admiring it*). Why, Gokul! This is indeed the best work you have ever done. Such precision!

GOKUL (bows). You want to try it on?

CHANDRAGUPTA. No need, no need! I am sure it fits. Gokul, you are by far the best darzi I have ever seen. I hope I will be doing business with you soon again. Here is your money. (GOKUL *bows.*) Thank you very much. In a single day! Most amazing. Namaste, Gokul. (*takes achkan on hanger and leaves, as* MISS KAPUR *enters*) Ah, Miss Kapur, namaste, and what a lovely day it is. (*exits down center aisle*)

GOKUL (*namastes*). Ah! Miss Kapur, this is a wonderful time of day to be seeing you. You are as the morning, as a rose.

MISS KAPUR (*giggles*). Oh, Gokul!

GOKUL. You want to see your salivar cumuz. Here it is just as you want it. (*gets blue salivar cumuz and hands it to her*)

MISS KAPUR (*holding it against her*). Oh! Oh! It is so beautiful! It is twice as pretty as that one in the magazine. (*twirls around*) Truly you are the best darzi in whole India!

GOKUL. Oh, Miss Kapur, you are flattering me. Truly I am not worthy. Many darzis are better than this humble one. I am a poor darzi.

MISS KAPUR. Don't be so modest. See! Perfection! A master-piece!

GOKUL (*bowing again*). Really, Miss Kapur, you are giving me too much credit.

MISS KAPUR. Nonsense! Now I must hurry. Namaste, Gokul. (*gestures*) Thank you again for such a beautiful, beautiful salivar cumuz.

GOKUL. You wish me to wrap it?

MISS KAPUR. No! I want to parade it everywhere so all people will see how so beautifully you sew! (*She turns to leave and meets* MRS. SINGH.) Ah, Mrs. Singh. See, see! Is it not the most lovely? (*exits*)

MRS. SINGH (*looking after her*). Really, such ill manners! (*turns to* GOKUL) But it is a beautiful salivar cumuz. I see, Gokul, you have been a very busy man this morning. I trust you are not so busy a man that you do not have my clothes ready.

GOKUL. Namaste, Mrs. Singh. (*gestures*) Your clothes are ready. I will wrap them now, if you wish. (*He gets brown paper from shelf and places it on platform.*)

MRS. SINGH (*examining each item as he wraps it*). Aah! Such magnificent work! This is the best work you have ever done! You have earned that title!

GOKUL. What title, Mrs. Singh?

MRS. SINGH (*pointing to sign above shop*) "Best Darzi in Whole India."

GOKUL. You give me too much honor. I am only one darzi. Not a very good darzi at that!

MRS. SINGH. Really, Gokul, I will never understand you. (*Her arms are piled now with packages.*) I must be going now. How much money are you asking?

GOKUL. Whatever you wish, Mrs. Singh.

MRS. SINGH. Now I am sure you have changed indeed! But this is truly fine work, and I am paying you what you deserve.

Namaste, Gokul. (*gestures*) And thank you. (*She departs with her packages.*)

GOKUL. Well, indeed, I know who did this. It was not I. For I am not a very good darzi . . . only a poor, boastful darzi. It was the little ones who never are seen, whom fortune sends to help those in need. I shall reward them. Every night they must have sweets and one bowl of curds. And every day I shall say one prayer for them. (*He goes off left and returns with bowl and dish of sweets. He places the bowl and the dish next to the sewing machine.*) And now I shall go and pray.

(GOKUL *exits down aisle. There is the sound of music and laughter.* RAM, LAL *and* MOHAN *enter right and dance as the curtain closes.*)

PRODUCTION NOTES

To suggest the busy atmosphere of the Indian bazaar, use a record of lively Indian film music.

There is no furniture in the shop; the characters sit on the platforms which are described in the setting of the play. Men sit cross-legged; women sit with their knees together.

Gokul wears baggy white pajamas. The shirt is made of thin muslin and has no collar. It buttons down the front and has long, loose sleeves. It is worn outside the pants and comes to about the thighs. His pants are fastened with a drawstring at the waist and are loose around the ankles. He is barefoot. He may have a mustache. Gokul's customers wear costumes which are similar to the ones they order. They all wear sandals.

Chandragupta Sahib wears an achkan, a fitted coat with a stand-up collar, long tight sleeves, and buttons down the front. It comes just below the knees. It may be brown or black. Underneath it he wears very tight, ankle-length pants. His hair is cut short, but he may wear a neatly trimmed mustache.

Miss Kapur is still young enough to wear a salivar cumuz and a chunee. When she is old enough to be married, she will wear a sari like Mrs. Singh's. The cumuz is a semifitted shirt (like a sheath) which comes to just above the knees. It has elbow-length sleeves. It may be a print or a Madras plaid. Beneath it she wears a salivar: loose, white pants with a fitted band at the ankles. The chunee is a long, flimsy scarf which is draped around her neck and floats behind her in the breeze. It is a color which matches the cumuz. Her hair is in a single long braid down her back.

Mrs. Singh, because she is older, wears a sari. This is a very long piece of cloth wrapped around the body so that one end hangs over the left shoulder. Both arms are left free. The sari may be any color except red, black or white. Underneath the sari is a floor-length petticoat and a choli: a tight short-sleeved blouse which leaves the midriff bare. Her long hair is knotted in a bun at the back of her neck.

The elves wear brown tights and leotards. They are barefoot. Their faces, hands and feet are as brown as their costumes. They wear tight brown caps to which pointed ears are attached. Their eyebrows are triangle-shaped. They dance to a record of folk music from northern India, or to the music of a backstage recorder. Here is an ancient Indian melody which might be appropriate for the recorder.

ANCIENT INDIAN MELODY

LONG AND SHORT DIVISION

LONG AND SHORT DIVISION

A dramatization based on the story "Melisande," by E. Nesbit,
which was first published in *Strand* magazine, July 1900,
and was included in *Nine Unlikely Tales*, by E. Nesbit, 1901.

CHARACTERS

THE KING *Robin*
THE QUEEN *Maureen*
THE PRINCESS, MELISANDE *Nancy*
THE ROYAL NURSE
THE ROYAL MATHEMATICIAN
THE HERALDS
THE PAGES
THE PARLOR MAID
THE RIGHT PRINCE, FLORIZEL *Carl*
THE WRONG PRINCES
THE WORST FAIRY, MALEVOLA
THE OTHER FAIRIES, GOOD AND BAD

*We are looking at the Royal Palace. Downstage left are steps
from the auditorium to an entrance arch. Downstage right is a
little balcony and a window, around which white roses climb.
These two corners of the stage are outside walls of the Palace.
The rest of the stage is the Big Room of the Palace. Upstage
center is a long table with a velvet cloth which covers it
completely to the floor. At the left end of the table is the* KING's
chair and at the right, the QUEEN's *chair. In front of the table is
a velvet bench, on which is a royal basket for the Royal Baby.
Behind the table is a curtained passageway. The curtains are
open in the center and make an upstage opening into the room.
Later the* PRINCESS's *chair will be there.*

You do not need a curtain for this play; if you use one, it opens to trumpet music, as two HERALDS *march down the aisle of the auditorium blowing long trumpets. They mount the steps to the entrance arch and stand, one on either side of it. The* ROYAL NURSE *follows, carrying the Royal Baby. Then come the* KING *and the* QUEEN *and the other members of the Royal Household. When the procession has gone through the archway into the Big Room, the music stops and the* HERALDS *enter the Palace. By this time the* ROYAL NURSE *has put the Royal Baby into the royal basket and has moved to stage right, so that the* QUEEN *and the* KING *can stand, hand in hand, with their backs to the audience, bending over the basket to admire their child. The rest of the Royal Household has disappeared into other unseen rooms.*

The KING *and* QUEEN *sigh deeply, then straighten up and look at each other and smile. The* KING *starts to kiss the* QUEEN, *who with her free hand beckons behind her to dismiss the* ROYAL NURSE. *The beaming* ROYAL NURSE *curtsies and backs out right, still looking at the happy Royal Couple.*

After the kiss, the KING *and* QUEEN *look again at the baby.*

QUEEN (*to baby*). Princess Melisande. (*She adores the name.*) You've had a lovely christening!

(*The* KING *and* QUEEN *smile at each other and sigh with pleasure.*)

KING (*moves to his chair, sits, says heartily*). How nice to be alone!

QUEEN (*starts to answer, hesitates, looks around the room, goes to her chair and sits*). Of course darling. Of course! But it does seem a LITTLE strange not to have a party.

KING. I'm sure we were right not to have one. I've seen too much trouble come of christening parties. However carefully you keep your guest book, some fairy or other is sure to get left out, and you know what THAT leads to.

QUEEN. Yes, dear, I know. My own cousin by marriage forgot some stuffy old fairy or other when she was sending out cards for her daughter's christening, and the old wretch turned up at the last moment, and the girl drops toads out of her mouth to this day. But still . . .

KING. Just so! And in my own family the most shocking things have occurred. The Fairy Malevola was not asked to my great-grandmother's christening, and you know . . .

QUEEN. Yes, dear, I know. The spindle and the hundred years' sleep. But still . . .

KING. None of that nonsense this time! No party! Not a single fairy invited, so NONE of them can be offended.

QUEEN. Unless they ALL are. . . . Gracious! What's happening?

(*What is happening is that down the aisle are coming* FAIRIES *of all ages, some beautiful, some ugly. They are chattering indignantly and making a great furor. The* KING *and* QUEEN *rise nervously and stand in front of the baby. The* FAIRIES, *led by* MALEVOLA, *sweep through the arch and into the room.*)

FAIRIES (*circling across the stage, facing the* KING *and* QUEEN.) Why didn't you ask ME to your christening party?????

KING (*roars*) SILENCE! (*It is now quiet, but threateningly so.*) We haven't had a party!

QUEEN (*about to cry, whispers to* KING). I told you so!

FAIRIES. You've had a christening!

QUEEN (*very sweetly*). I'm terribly sorry but . . .

MALEVOLA (*going to* QUEEN *and shaking her finger*). Don't begin to make excuses! That only makes your conduct worse!

OTHER FAIRIES. Much worse!

MALEVOLA. You know well enough what happens if a fairy is left out of a christening party!

OTHER FAIRIES. You know!!

MALEVOLA. We are all going to give our christening presents now!

OTHER FAIRIES. Now!!!

MALEVOLA. As the fairy of highest social position, I shall begin. The Princess SHALL BE BALD!

(*The sobbing* QUEEN *sits in her chair. Triumphant* MALEVOLA *goes back into the fairy circle.*)

SECOND FAIRY (*stepping forward*). The Princess SHALL . . .

KING (*steps to her and shouts*). No you don't! (*There is a shocked silence; then the* KING *continues quietly*). I wonder at you, ladies; I do indeed. How can you be so unfairylike? Has none of you been to school? Has none of you studied history?

SECOND FAIRY. How dare you? It is my turn, and I say the Princess . . .

KING (*puts his hand over her mouth*). I won't have it! Listen to reason, or you'll be sorry! You all know that a fairy who breaks the traditions of history goes out—like a candle! And besides, all tradition shows that only ONE bad fairy is ever forgotten at a christening party and the good ones are always invited; so either this is not a christening party, or else you were all invited except one, and by her own admission that one was Malevola. It nearly always is. She has been left out of more christening parties than all the rest of you put together. Do I make myself clear?

FAIRIES (*put their chins in their hands to think, and then murmur in a descending scale*). Hmmmmmmmmmmmmmmmm.

THIRD FAIRY. Perhaps there IS something in what His Majesty says.

KING. If you don't believe me, give your nasty gifts to my innocent child. But as sure as you do, out you go—like a candle flame! Will you risk it?

THIRD FAIRY (*goes to* QUEEN *and says sweetly*). What a lovely party it has been. I really must be going!

QUEEN (*rises, a gracious hostess, and gives her hand to the fairy*). Thank you.

(*The other* FAIRIES, *except* MALEVOLA, *circle, following the leader, and shake hands with the* QUEEN *before they depart.*)

FAIRIES (*each one says something ladies say when they leave parties*). A delightful afternoon . . . A beautiful baby . . . Such lovely refreshments . . . Couldn't have been nicer . . . Can't thank you enough . . . (*etc.*)

SECOND FAIRY (*the last of the line-up*). DO ask us again soon, dear Queen. I shall be so LONGING to see you again, and the DEAR baby! (*She is followed off by* MALEVOLA, *who exits with an evil cackle.*)

(*The* QUEEN *bends over the baby, weeping. The* KING *goes to her.*)

KING. Don't cry, my love. I have a wish lying by, which I've never had occasion to use. My Fairy Godmother gave it to me for a wedding present, but since I married you I've had nothing to wish for!

QUEEN (*through her tears*). Thank you, dear.

KING. I'll keep the wish till Melisande grows up. Then I'll give it to her, and if she wants to wish for hair she can.

QUEEN. Won't you please wish for it now?

KING. No, dearest. She may want something else more when she grows up.

QUEEN. I shall sew beautiful little caps for her to wear until then.

(KING *picks up the basket and carries it off right; the sad* QUEEN *follows him.*

The lights fade out; there is music to indicate time passing. A PAGE *enters up right and places the* PRINCESS'S *chair up center, back of the table. Another* PAGE *enters right and places the Royal Sewing Box on the bench below the table. They bow to the audience and depart. The* QUEEN *enters, stage right. She goes to the sewing box and takes from it some pale green silk and a needle and thread. Then she sits in her chair and sews, as the lights rise and the music fades.)*

KING (*enters right followed by a* PAGE *who carries an inkpot and quill pen*). Good morning, my love! (*kisses her on top of her head*) That's a lovely cap—the prettiest you've made yet! (*He sits in his chair and writes on parchment, dipping the quill pen in the inkpot the* PAGE *holds.*)

QUEEN. Thank you, dear. It's the six hundredth one in these sixteen years. (*They sit silently, each at his work. Then the* QUEEN *stops sewing.*) My love, Melisande is old enough to know what she wants. Let her have the wish!

KING (*smiling*). Exactly! I was going to surprise you. I am writing to my Fairy Godmother to ask her permission to give it away. (*reads*) "I have never had occasion to use it, though it has always made me happy to know that I had such a thing in the house. The wish is as good as new, and my daughter is now of an age to appreciate so valuable a present." (*He signs his name with a flourish and hands the parchment to the* PAGE.) Send it by the fastest butterfly!

(*The* PAGE *bows and runs off left. The* QUEEN, *who has risen joyfully, goes to the* KING *and embraces him. She runs back to pick up her sewing and to jam it into the sewing box.*)

QUEEN (*running off right, with sewing box*). Melisande! Melisande!

HERALD (*appearing at balcony window down right*). Princess Melisande! Princess Melisande!

SECOND HERALD (*appearing in arch down left*). Princess Melisande!

(*The* PARLOR MAID *scurries through from right and off left, pausing briefly to curtsy to the* KING. *The* ROYAL NURSE *scurries across the stage from left to right.*

MELISANDE, *who is a beautiful girl in a pretty cap and dress, runs down the right aisle of the auditorium. She carries flowers, and holds up her long skirts as she runs.*)

MELISANDE (*calling gaily*). Coming! Coming! (*She waves to the* HERALD *on the balcony, as she passes below him to the arch, left. She nods to the* HERALD *in the archway, runs up the steps and enters the big room. She runs to her father, curtsies to him and then hugs him.*) What is it, Father? Everyone is scurrying so! Is there a surprise?

(*The* QUEEN *runs in from right, followed by the* ROYAL NURSE *and the* HERALD *who has been on balcony. The* PARLOR MAID *and the other* HERALD *run in from left.*)

QUEEN. My darling child! (*to* KING) Has the butterfly returned?

MELISANDE. I saw such a lovely one. Look what it dropped into my flowers in the garden. (*She pulls a tiny note out of a flower.*)

KING (*takes note and reads*). "Dear King: Pray do whatever you like with my poor little present. I had quite forgotten it, but I am pleased to think that you have treasured it all these years. Your affectionate Godmother, Fortuna."

MELISANDE. Father, TELL me!

QUEEN. Darling, all these years your father has had . . .

KING. Darling, all these years your father has had a surprise for you. I have had an unused wish, which my Fairy Godmother gave me at my wedding. I have been saving it for you. You may have it now. (*to* PAGE) Bring my small safe.

(*The* PAGE *bows and exits right.* MELISANDE *stands, stage center, thinking happily. The* PAGE *returns with a small gold safe on a tray. He places this at the end of table in front of the* KING. *The* KING *takes a key from several which hang on his belt, opens the safe, takes out the wish— which looks like a small soap bubble.*)

KING. For you, my dear.

MELISANDE (*takes it carefully, holds it up. She stands on tiptoe and closes her eyes.*) I wish that all my Father's subjects should be QUITE HAPPY!

(*The* QUEEN *catches her breath in dismay. There is a pause.* MELISANDE *opens her eyes and looks at the wish.*)

MELISANDE. It did not go off.

ROYAL NURSE. It did not go off, Your Majesties, because all of your subjects are already happy.

OTHER ATTENDANTS (*bowing*). Yes, Your Majesties.

KING AND QUEEN (*bowing to them*). Thank you.

QUEEN. Dearest Melisande, you can make another wish. Please, darling, this time . . .

KING. Tut, tut, my dearest love. It is HER wish.

MELISANDE (*repeating the same action*). I wish that all my Father's subjects should be GOOD. (*Pause. She opens her eyes.*) It did not go off.

KING. It did not go off because all of our subjects are already good.

(*The* KING *and* QUEEN *bow to their attendants.*)

ATTENDANTS (*returning the bow*). Thank you, Your Majesties.

QUEEN. Dearest Melisande, for my sake, wish what I tell you.

MELISANDE. Why, of course I will, Mother. (*The* QUEEN *whispers to her.*) I wish I had golden hair a yard long, and that it would grow an inch every day, and grow twice as fast every time it was cut, and . . .

KING. Stop!

(*Bang! The lights go off. When they come on, gold dust is streaming from the wish, and* MELISANDE *is smiling through a shower of golden hair.*)

QUEEN. How beautiful! What a pity you interrupted her, dear; she hadn't finished.

KING. What was the end?

MELISANDE. I was only going to say, "and twice as thick."

KING. It's a very good thing you didn't. You've done about enough.

QUEEN. Why, what's the matter?

KING. You'll know soon enough. Come, let's be happy while we may. Give me a kiss, Melisande, and then ask the Nurse to teach you how to comb your hair.

MELISANDE (*going to him for a kiss*). I know how. I've often combed Mother's.

KING. Your Mother has beautiful hair. I fancy you will find your own less easy to manage.

QUEEN. Come, darling! (*She strokes the golden hair as she takes* MELISANDE *off right, followed by the* NURSE *and the* PARLOR MAID.)

KING (*to the others*). You all may go. Send me the Royal Mathematician.

OTHERS. Yes, Your Majesty. (*bow and off left*)

(*The* KING *paces and mutters as he counts on his fingers.*)

ROYAL MATHEMATICIAN (*enters left and bows*). You sent for me, Your Majesty?

KING. My daughter's hair is now a yard long. If it grows an inch every night . . .

ROYAL MATHEMATICIAN. It will be two yards long in about five weeks.

KING. Then it will trail on the floor and sweep up all the dust. When it is three yards long . . .

ROYAL MATHEMATICIAN. It will be quite uncomfortable.

KING. And if she cuts it off when it is three yards long because it is so uncomfortable, it will grow twice as fast as before, so . . .

ROYAL MATHEMATICIAN. So that in 36 days it will be as long again.

KING. And if she cuts it off again, it will grow four times as fast . . .

ROYAL MATHEMATICIAN. So that in 18 days it will be as long again.

KING. And if she cuts it then . . .

ROYAL MATHEMATICIAN (*computing rapidly*). It will grow 8 inches a day, and the next time it is cut it will grow 16 inches a day, and then next time 32 inches a day and then 64 inches a day and then 128 inches a day, and so on.

KING. So that by that time if she cuts her hair short at night so that she can sleep, she will wake up in the morning with so much hair she will not be able to move and will have to have it cut off before she can get out of bed.

ROYAL MATHEMATICIAN. And that would mean . . .

(*The* KING *has walked off left, head in hands. The* ROYAL MATHEMATICIAN, *still computing, follows him.*
Lights dim. Music plays. Time passes. The lights come up and the KING is entering from left, followed by the QUEEN.*)

QUEEN (*as she follows him*). Darling, what shall we do? She has to cut it at night in order to get INTO her bed, and by morning it has to be cut again in order that she get OUT of her bed, and the problem of what to DO with the hair we cut OFF, beautiful as it is. . . .(*He continues to pace and she continues to talk as she follows him.*) I have sent bracelets and belts of it to all my relations. . . .

KING. And my merchants are exporting pillows and mattresses stuffed with it, and all the sailors in the world are using ropes made of it. In fact our country is quite wealthy because of it; it is our most staple export. . . .

QUEEN. All of the palaces have curtains made of it. . . .

KING. And the hermits are making their hairshirts of it. . . .

QUEEN. And all well-born infants have little warm wrappers of it. . . .

KING (*sits wearily on bench in front of table*). I have written to my Fairy Godmother to see if something cannot be done.

QUEEN (*immediately happy*). Darling, WHY didn't you do that SOONER?

(*The* KING *looks at her and is about to speak when the* PAGE *enters.*)

PAGE (*bowing*). Your Majesty, the skylark has just returned with this.

KING (*takes letter and reads, as* QUEEN *peers over his shoulder*). "Why not . . ."

QUEEN. " . . . advertise for a competent Prince? Offer the usual reward."

KING. I'll write the advertisement immediately. (*He rises and starts off right.*)

QUEEN. I'll help you! (*She runs after him.*)

HERALDS (*instantly appearing from the palace at archway down left*). ANY RESPECTABLE PRINCE WITH PROPER

REFERENCES SHALL MARRY THE PRINCESS MELISANDE IF HE CAN STOP HER HAIR FROM GROWING!

(They proclaim the announcement twice. Then they come down the steps from the arch, cross in front of audience, and circle up left aisle to rear of audience, still proclaiming.

From the rear, down the left aisle, comes the Procession of PRINCES. *Each one carries a bottle or a box. This is a pantomime scene with music throughout.* MELISANDE *appears at window of balcony. Masses of hair are piled behind her head. Each* PRINCE *comes across stage, stands in front of window, gives her his bottle or box, hesitates as she drinks or eats, then sadly goes off up aisle.*

After they have all come and gone, as the lights have been dimming, MELISANDE *is still at her window. The music stops and all is quiet. A moon shines on the* PRINCESS.

PRINCE FLORIZEL *comes down the aisle. He carries a large covered something. He stands below the window in the moonlight and looks up at* MELISANDE.)

FLORIZEL *(softly)*. Are you Melisande?

MELISANDE. Yes, and you are . . .

FLORIZEL. Florizel.

MELISANDE *(softly)*. Florizel!

FLORIZEL. There are many roses round your window.

MELISANDE. Here is one for you. *(She tosses him a rose.)*

FLORIZEL. If I can do what your father asks, will you marry me?

MELISANDE. He has promised that I shall.

FLORIZEL. His promise is nothing to me. I want yours. Will you give it to me?

MELISANDE (*tossing another rose*). Yes.

FLORIZEL. I want your hand. . . .

MELISANDE (*another rose*). Yes.

FLORIZEL. And your heart with it.

MELISANDE (*another rose*). Yes.

FLORIZEL. (*He has put down his big package. He holds up his arms to her.*) Will you come to me?

MELISANDE. But my hair!

FLORIZEL. Let it flow through the window back of you. I know you cannot turn around. Come!

> (FLORIZEL *braces himself and reaches up to her as she steps carefully over the low railing into his arms. He lowers her to the ground. Her hair streams behind her through the window into the palace.* FLORIZEL *kneels and kisses her hand.*)

MELISANDE. Florizel . . . But what can we do?

FLORIZEL. If you trust me, stay here quietly and do not be afraid.

MELISANDE. I trust you.

> (FLORIZEL *picks up the covered package, goes into the Palace and then appears on the balcony.*)

FLORIZEL. I am here just above you, Melisande. Do not be frightened, even if it hurts a little.

MELISANDE. Yes, Florizel.

> (FLORIZEL *uncovers a reel and starts winding her hair on it. As he turns the wheel, there is a clicking noise and the hair winds onto the reel.*)

FLORIZEL. It is almost time, Melisande. Tell me when I have stretched your hair until I have just pulled your feet off the ground!

MELISANDE (*now on tiptoe, her hair straight up*). Now, Florizel!

(FLORIZEL *stops turning the crank. He holds tightly to her hair with one hand, leans over the balcony, and with the other hand draws his sword across the hair. Then he gently lets her down by her hair until her feet touch and she falls on the ground. Instantly he jumps down to her. He helps her stand, and then kneels to her.*)

MELISANDE. Florizel! But won't it grow again?

FLORIZEL. I think not, Melisande! And now that I have your hand and heart, let us find your father and receive his blessing.

MELISANDE. It is almost morning. Come! (*She leads him into the big room of the Palace.*) Stay here. I want to tell them first (*She runs off right, stopping to throw him a kiss.*)

(*The light increases.* PAGES *enter from left with breakfast dishes. They are surprised to see a visitor; but life has been rather surprising lately, so they simply bow to him and set an extra place at the table.* FLORIZEL *walks down left to stand and dream. The lights are up full now. A* PAGE *stands behind each of the three chairs.*

MELISANDE *runs in and goes to* FLORIZEL. *She is followed by the* QUEEN, *who rushes to him and embraces him. The* KING *follows.*)

QUEEN. Florizel, this is the most glorious day of our life! (*He kneels and kisses her hand.*) Her hair hasn't grown since you cut it, and it's BEEN growing at the rate of . . .

KING (*putting his hands on his wife's shoulders and moving her a bit*). Stand up, my boy! Let me shake your hand. (*does so*) How did you do it?

QUEEN. Sit down with us and tell us all about it. (*She goes to her chair and speaks to her* PAGE.) Set a place for the Prince, please.

ALL PAGES (*bowing*). We did, Your Majesty.

(MELISANDE *goes to her chair behind the table and sits.* KING *sits in his chair.* FLORIZEL *sits on bench below table.*)

KING (*as the three* PAGES *bend forward to uncover dishes and the sitters spread their napkins*). Now, my boy, tell us how you did it!

FLORIZEL (*modestly*). The simplest thing in the world. You have always cut the HAIR off the PRINCESS. I just cut the PRINCESS off the HAIR.

QUEEN. You . . . you did WHAT? I didn't quite understand. . . .

FLORIZEL. I cut the PRINCESS off the HAIR.

MELISANDE (*laughing*). Mother, don't you see? He didn't cut my HAIR off, he cut ME off!

KING (*looking gravely at his daughter*). Humph!

MELISANDE (*excitedly*). Mother dearest, I CANNOT sit here on such a morning and eat my breakfast. May I please go sit beside Florizel?

QUEEN. Of course, darling. I can remember when I was your age, I . . .

KING (*shaking his finger at her*). Don't start that, my dear!

(MELISANDE *rises. She is several inches taller than she was.*)

QUEEN (*looking at her curiously*). Melisande, you seem . . . different . . . taller. . . .

KING (*sadly*). I feared as much. (*He rises, as does* FLORIZEL. *By now* MELISANDE *is another several inches taller.*)

QUEEN (*burying her head in her hands*). Ohhhhhhhh! Whatever is the matter?

KING (*more sadly*). I feared as much. (*puts his hand on* FLORI-ZEL's *shoulder*) You see, my poor Florizel, when we cut the

HAIR off, IT grows; so when we cut the PRINCESS off, SHE grows. I wish you had happened to think of THAT!

MELISANDE. But if I don't stop, I will soon bump the ceiling. Ohhhh!

(*She runs off behind the curtain up left, growing taller as she goes.*)

FLORIZEL. Melisande! Stop! Where are you going?

MELISANDE (*off*). Outdoors!

(FLORIZEL *rushes off stage left, followed by the* QUEEN.)

KING (*slowly*). I wonder what will be the rate of progression!

(*The* PAGES, *forgetting their manners, start off after the* QUEEN. *The* KING *catches one of them by the arm.*)

KING. Bring ink and parchment and be quick about it!

PAGE (*bowing meekly*). Yes, Your Majesty. (*runs off right. The* KING *sits at the table and thinks. The* PAGE *returns with parchment and quill.* KING *writes*)

KING. There! Send that by flying-fish!

PAGE. Yes, Your Majesty! (*He rushes off left, forgetting to bow.*)

QUEEN (*returns, weeping, and crosses to her chair to sit*). She is sitting in the garden and she is already almost as high as the castle tower! Everything she has on has grown with her and . . .

KING. Well, that at least is SOMETHING to be thankful for! Her clothes still fit!

QUEEN. The little pincushion at her waist is as big as a toadstool, and her little golden scissors are as big as crossed swords.

FLORIZEL (*rushing in*). Where is the circular stairway to the tower?

QUEEN. To the tower? (*gestures right*) That way and across the drawbridge . . .

KING (*suspiciously*). Why? Do you have ANOTHER idea?

FLORIZEL (*as he goes*). If she can hear me, I will tell her to cut off her hair with her giant scissors. (*He races off right.*)

KING (*rises*). What an impetuous young man!

QUEEN (*radiantly*). But of course! Then she will stop growing. . . .

KING. Perhaps. But then?

PARLOR MAID (*runs in and curtsies*). Madam, dear Queen, come see! The Princess is cutting her hair and she is shrinking. . . .

FLORIZEL (*runs back in from right*). It's working! It's working! (*He dashes off left, followed by the* QUEEN *and the* PARLOR MAID.)

PARLOR MAID (*returning breathless*). Your Majesty, she's normal and she's stopped! And I forgot to give you this! (*She hands the* KING *a note and dashes out again.*)

(*Before the* KING *can read the note, there is a shout of joy off left. The* QUEEN *comes in, laughing and crying. She is followed by* FLORIZEL *and* MELISANDE. MELISANDE *has no hair showing at all under her headdress.*)

QUEEN (*sits in her chair and fans herself*). What a day it has been!

MELISANDE. Father, my dear Prince has saved me! He told me what to do. And now I am my proper size again.

KING (*rubbing his chin*). My dear young man, my dear BRILLIANT young man, don't you see that we're just where we were before? Melisande's hair is undoubtedly growing already.

MELISANDE (*puts her hands to her headdress and wails*). It IS! I can feel it! (*She runs off right, holding her hands to her head.*)

QUEEN (*running after her*). No, no no!

(FLORIZEL *sinks to the bench. He sits with his elbows on his knees, his head in his hands.*)

KING (*opens the note and reads*). "Sorry for your troubles. Why not try scales?" Scales?

FLORIZEL (*looking straight out at audience*). Scales . . . ? Scales?? (*He rises.*) SCALES!!! Your Highness, I've GOT it! I want all the palace workmen immediately! (*He strides off left, leaving a skeptical* KING.)

(*Lights and music. Attendants bring on stage giant balance scales and place them center.* FLORIZEL *directs them. The* ROYAL MATHEMATICIAN *measures. The* KING *watches.*)

FLORIZEL (*as the lights come up full*). Now! We are ready! Will you bring Melisande?

KING. Are you speaking to me? Will I . . . ? Well, yes, I'll get her. (*goes off right*)

(FLORIZEL *and* ROYAL MATHEMATICIAN *make sure the scales are perfectly balanced.* MELISANDE *enters slowly. Her hair hangs loose to her feet and the* NURSE, *the* QUEEN *and the* PARLOR MAID *carry the rest of the hair wound into a big twisted roll which extends beyond them on the floor to offstage right.* FLORIZEL *meets* MELISANDE *and leads her behind the scales to the left side. The women arrange the long roll of her hair on the floor behind the center of the scales platform. They pile it up as well as they can, but there is still a long roll of it continuing on the floor to off right.*)

FLORIZEL. My darling Melisande, will you trust me entirely and get into this gold scale?

MELISANDE. What is going into the other scale?

FLORIZEL. Your hair. You see, when your hair is cut off you, IT grows; and when you are cut off your hair, YOU grow. But if, when your hair is no more than you and you are no more than your hair, I snip between you and it, then neither you nor your hair can possibly decide which ought to go on growing.

MELISANDE. Suppose BOTH did.

FLORIZEL. Impossible. There are limits even to Malevola's malevolence. Besides your father's Fairy Godmother said "Scales." Will you try it?

MELISANDE. I will do whatever you wish. But let me kiss my Father and Mother once and Nurse and you too, my dear, in case I grow large again and can kiss nobody any more.

(*One by one they come to kiss her. Then the* QUEEN, *the* NURSE *and the* PARLOR MAID *start busily packing hair into the scale, right; the* KING *and the* PAGES *help* MELISANDE *into the scale, left.* FLORIZEL *stands upstage center facing the scales, with his sword drawn. The* ROYAL MATHEMA-TICIAN, *his back to the audience, stands downstage center with his hand raised.*)

ROYAL MATHEMATICIAN (*when the pointer indicates an exact balance*). NOW!!

(FLORIZEL'S *sword flashes. The hair is cut.* FLORIZEL *and the* KING *help* MELISANDE *out of her scale. As they do so, the other scale bumps down on the ground. The women have rushed to the* PRINCESS, *whose lovely hair is just down to her pretty ankles.*

There is nothing left now except the blessing. This is, of course, a tableau. The KING *and* QUEEN *are down center, right; the* PRINCE *and* PRINCESS *kneel facing them. The others may arrange themselves in any effective way.*)

KING (*his hand raised to bless them*). May you live happily ever after! You are a young man of sound judgment!

(*As the lights dim and the curtain starts to close, we can hear the words of the* ROYAL MATHEMATICIAN.)

ROYAL MATHEMATICIAN· Since the scales are 10 feet and 10½ inches apart, her hair is now 5 feet and 5¼ inches long.

PRODUCTION NOTES

If you are tired of old-fashioned fairy tales and are tired of mathematics, here is a play which has some fun with both subjects. It is satire and, like all good satire, it is played completely seriously.

There are many characters in the play, but the casting is flexible. Actors who have time to change costumes can take more than one part. There can be any number of Pages, Heralds, Wrong Princes, Fairies. The Procession of Princes could be omitted and lines inserted to inform the audience that many had come and failed.

The set can be drapes, screens, flats or a combination of these. If it is impracticable to have an archway flat and a balcony flat to indicate the opposite sides of the palace, these could be omitted; in which case, the window could be in the interior of the palace on the left side of the big room. The Princess could stand behind it on a high box or stepladder.

There are several production tricks which must be carefully managed. How does Melisande grow taller on stage? She steps first on a box a few inches lower than her chair, then on the seat of her chair, then on a long bench which is against the left side of the chair seat and a bit higher. This bench slants up to the left, and its left end is behind the alcove curtain. The entire structure is hidden from the front by a table covered with a floor-length tablecloth.

How does the hair grow long and short? Melisande wears an elaborate headdress which conceals a wig of hair which when

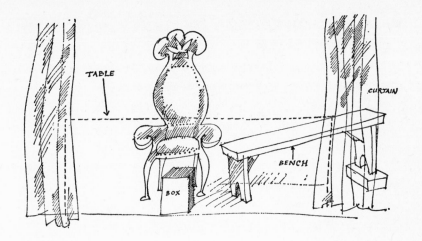

exposed will hang to her ankles. Make the wig by raveling long thick rope, or by fringing long yellow crepe paper. Sew this false hair to a skullcap and then sew the cap securely inside the headdress. Attach a floor-length veil to the sides and back of the headdress, so that when the hair hangs down it is under a veil and is not seen directly; this will make it look less artificial. When the wish explodes and the lights go off, Melisande shakes the hair down so that it hangs loose. In the balcony scene her hair hangs loose, and behind it are rolls of fake hair which are later used in the scales scene. When she enters for breakfast, her hair hangs loose. When she comes back from growing tall, the hair is tucked under the headdress. In the last scene, the hair hangs loose. The women carry long rolls of hair, made of the same material, which seem to be attached to the hanging hair. They place the rolls of hair back of the scales platform; the Prince only pretends to cut it.

What do you use for the wish? Get a plastic Easter egg which opens in the middle and fill it with glitter dust.

How do you make the scales? These are balancing scales which hang from a crosspiece, which is supported by a center upright braced from the rear to stand erect. The upright is covered with a triangular piece of painted cardboard, at the top of which is fastened a pointer. The pointer does not really have to move, since the Mathematician who stands in front of the scales covers the pointer from the view of the audience. Attach to the base of the upright a piece of cardboard which looks like a platform base. This hides the hair on the floor behind it, so the Prince's motion of cutting is enough to make the audience believe that he actually cuts the hair. The two scales can be of beaverboard or any material strong enough not to tear or break. Fasten around the seat of each scale a floor-length ruffle which will look decorative. This ruffle conceals a box attached to the scale in which the Princess sits. The box rests on the floor and supports her weight. Put foam rubber under the box, so that the scale will spring a little as she sits and rises.

OLD PIPES

OLD PIPES

Dramatized from the story
"Old Pipes and the Dryad," by Frank R. Stockton.
The story was first published by Charles Scribner's Sons
in Stockton's book, *The Queen's Museum*.

Characters

In this play there are two kinds of characters, the people ones
and the magic ones. The ECHO-DWARFS live in the mountains
and each ECHO-DWARF has his own special job. The FIDDLER
ECHO-DWARF's job is to echo the sound of the fiddle; the PIPES
ECHO-DWARF echoes the sound of the pipes, etc. These parts
will be played, of course, by your smallest actors. The villagers
do not notice the dwarfs; only the audience sees how the echoes
are really made.

THE PEOPLE CHARACTERS	THE MAGIC CHARACTERS
FIDDLER	FIDDLER ECHO-DWARF
OLD PIPES, A VERY OLD MAN	PIPES ECHO-DWARF
HIS MOTHER, A VERY, VERY	SINGER ECHO-DWARF
OLD WOMAN	CHILDREN'S SHOUTS ECHO-
ELLEN, ABOUT EIGHT YEARS	DWARF
OLD	OTHER ECHO-DWARFS
COLIN, HER BROTHER, ABOUT	THE DRYAD
TEN	
MARIE, ABOUT TWELVE	
MARTIN, HER BROTHER, ABOUT	
ELEVEN	
OTHER CHILDREN OF THE	
VILLAGE	

*The scene is in a mountainous countryside with high meadows,
like Switzerland. Downstage right is a clearing at the edge of a*

village, which is offstage. A path leads through the clearing, up a rocky hillside, past a giant oak tree and past the porch of a little cottage. The cottage itself, off up left, we do not see. Behind the steep path are jagged mountains, on one of which is a ledge big enough to hold a sleeping dwarf. There is a dwarf asleep there now. He is PIPES ECHO-DWARF, *a very fat lazy little fellow, who is so quietly sleeping that he seems only a part of the scenery.*

OLD PIPES *has just come out of his cottage and has turned back to wave to his* MOTHER *before he starts down the hill to the village. He walks carefully, pausing frequently to rest. As he nears the village he stops to watch and to listen, as the* FIDDLER *enters from down right, playing a tune. The* FIDDLER ECHO-DWARF *sticks his head over a mountain crag and echoes the notes of the fiddle. Several* CHILDREN *run on from down right. They are laughing and clapping. The* CHILDREN'S SHOUTS ECHO-DWARF *and other* ECHO-DWARFS *stick their heads over the mountain and echo the shouts, laughter and clapping. Two of the* CHILDREN *sing the* FIDDLER'S *tune, and the* SINGER ECHO-DWARF *echoes the song.* PIPES ECHO-DWARF, *on his ledge, stretches, yawns, covers his ears, and goes back to sleep.* OLD PIPES *has been listening happily, nodding his head in time to the music. Now he makes his way through the* CHILDREN, *who greet him with smiles and nods. He goes off right into the village.*

FIDDLER (*ending his tune with a gay flourish*). That's all now. Run along home, you!

(*The* CHILDREN, *except* ELLEN *and* COLIN, *run off down right. As their voices fade, their* ECHO-DWARFS *disappear behind the mountain.*)

ELLEN. Let's go up the mountain, Colin, and meet Marie and Martin.

COLIN. No, let's wait here for them. (*He flops down on the ground.*)

FIDDLER. They won't be along until sunset, when they've started the cows down. I hear the bells now. Listen!

(*From off up left there is a faint tinkling of bells with even fainter bell-echoes.*)

ELLEN. Yes! The cows are going down the longer, easy path.

COLIN. Marie and Martin will race down over the rocks, though.

ELLEN. What a fun job they have!

COLIN. When they get too old to do it, maybe you and I can get the job.

ELLEN. Oh, I wish we could! How did they get to do it? Because their father is the mayor? Who did it before them?

COLIN. Of course they got the job because their father is the mayor, but NO one did it before Marie and Martin. You know that!

ELLEN (*doubtfully*). Of course I know that. But I've forgotten WHY no one did it before them. And don't be so smarty. We did have COWS before!

FIDDLER (*improvising a little song, which is echoed by his* ECHO-DWARF).

Forever and ever since hills began
And meadows were fresh with flowers,
Our cows have climbed to the sunny heights
In spring and summer hours.

ELLEN. Yes . . . and it was Old Pipes, of course, forever and ever who piped them down. I DO remember.

FIDDLER. Well forever and ever is a long time. But Old Pipes could pipe a bird out of a tree, a cow out of the highest meadow, a star out of the sky.

COLIN. And he still thinks he does!

FIDDLER. That's the pity of it. He still thinks he does. And the village fathers pay him for thinking he does it.

ELLEN. When it's really Marie and Martin who bring the cows down.

FIDDLER. When it's really Marie and Martin who bring the cows down. He's grown so old and his piping is so feeble now that it doesn't reach the high meadows. But he doesn't know it, and he pipes every evening.

COLIN. And his mother doesn't know it either, because she's even OLDER.

ELLEN. Oho, Mr. Smarty! Mr. Pipes's Mother is older than her son?

COLIN. You know what I mean. She is almost deaf and almost blind and she is just older than ANYthing. Imagine Old Pipes still having a mother!

FIDDLER. Well, they're both very old. But of course time is—ahem—relevant. YOU two are young.

ELLEN. What does "time is—ahem—relevant" mean?

FIDDLER (*laughing*). One thing it means is that you've forgotten his piping, although it was only two years ago that the cows stopped hearing him. But I remember it as clearly as yesterday.

ELLEN. Hmm. I see, I guess. But I was only five and you were . . .

FIDDLER. Exactly! The most beautiful sound of the day it was. From his cottage up there he'd pipe, and down in the village we'd hear the clear sounds, and the echoes filling the valley, and we'd stop to listen. Soon we'd hear the distant, distant tinkle of the bells. We'd know that the breathing of a day had finished and a summer evening was starting.

ELLEN (*after a moment*). But why doesn't someone else pipe them now, if he's too old?

FIDDLER. And what would become of Old Pipes, who is too feeble for other work and who is paid by the village to pipe the cows?

COLIN. He's gone now to get his pay, as he does every week. (*happily*) I like our village.

ELLEN (*happily*). I like our village too.

FIDDLER. It's a long hard climb for him, back to his home. . . .

ELLEN and COLIN. To his mother! (*They laugh.*)

VOICE (*off down right calling, and being echoed from the mountain*). Colin! Ellen!

FIDDLER (*laughing*). And you two had best get back home to YOUR Mother! You might get kissed by a dryad on an evening like this one!

ELLEN and COLIN. Oh, no!

FIDDLER. On summer days when the moon rises before the sun goes down, dryads can come out of their trees if anyone can find the keys which lock them in. And if a dryad kisses you, it makes you ten years younger, you know.

ELLEN. A dryad had better not kiss me!

FIDDLER. I wish one would kiss ME! That's what I mean about time is relevant.

VOICE (*and echo*). Colin!! Ellen!!

COLIN. Coming, Mother! (*takes* ELLEN'*s hand*) Come on! (*They start off right.*)

OLD PIPES (*entering right. He carries a little pouch of money*). A lovely evening to you!

ELLEN and COLIN. And to you, Old Pipes! (*They run off.*)

OLD PIPES. It's the witching time of year, and every evening is lovelier than the one before.

FIDDLER. You've a long climb back up the hill, Old Pipes.

OLD PIPES. A long climb but a joyous one, because I've done my week's work well. I save my strength for this climb all week. To make it even more joyous, fiddle me a bit of the way. I wish Mother could hear your fiddling.

FIDDLER. Your mother's old for hearing fiddling, Old Pipes.

OLD PIPES (*chuckling*). She's older than that! But I'll tell her about it and she'll say she heard it. Who knows, indeed, what's truth and what's fancy?

(OLD PIPES *starts slowly up the hill, as the* FIDDLER *plays the beginning of a tune, which his* ECHO-DWARF *echoes. The* FIDDLER *and the* ECHO *stop, but* OLD PIPES *keeps time to imaginary music as he climbs.*)

FIDDLER (*watching* OLD PIPES). Who knows what's truth and what's fancy? (*He goes off down right.*)

(OLD PIPES *is halfway up the hill now. He sits to rest at the right of the giant oak tree.* MARTIN *runs on from up left, followed by* MARIE. *They do not see* OLD PIPES.)

MARIE. Slow down a minute, Martin, and let me catch my breath! Whew, I'm tired!

MARTIN. Aren't we lucky to have such a fine job! It must have been about two years ago that Father decided the cattle couldn't hear Old Pipes and we got the job.

MARIE. Don't talk so loud, Martin. He lives just up there, you know, and it would be terrible if he knew we were doing the job he thinks he does each day. Come on, I'm rested now!

(MARIE *and* MARTIN *run past the oak tree and see* OLD PIPES. *They are embarrassed.*)

OLD PIPES. It's a lovely evening, children.

MARIE AND MARTIN. Yes, sir.

MARIE. You look very tired, sir.

OLD PIPES. I am very tired and I've still a bit of the way to go.

MARTIN. Please may we help you? Give me your hand. (*He helps* OLD PIPES *up.*)

MARIE. Here! I'll pull and Martin you push. (*She takes* OLD PIPES's *hands and* MARTIN *gets behind* OLD PIPES. *They go up the hill with him and are soon at the porch of the cottage.*)

OLD PIPES. Thank you, children. Now run along fast before it is dark.

MARIE. Good night, dear Old Pipes.

(*The children start down the hill.* OLD PIPES, *motionless, looks after them.*)

MARIE (*softly*). Oh, Martin, I hope he didn't hear what we said!

MARTIN. I hope not! I don't think he did, though; he didn't mention it.

MARIE. But he looked sad, Martin!

MARTIN (*uneasily*). Come on, Marie. (*loudly*) Last one home's a . . . (*His voice trails off as he races off down right.*)

MARIE (*racing after him and off*). No fair, Martin . . .

(*There is a pause. Then* OLD PIPES *turns to the cottage.*)

OLD PIPES (*shouting*). Mother! (*louder*) Mother!!

MOTHER (*coming onto porch*). Oh, you're back, son. Was it a good walk to the village?

OLD PIPES (*shouting*). Two children helped me up the hill.

MOTHER (*nodding*). That's nice. They should have come in to see me.

OLD PIPES (*shouting into her ear*). They were tired because they had been bringing in the cows from the mountain.

MOTHER. Why?

OLD PIPES. The cattle can't hear my pipes any more and those children bring the cattle down every day.

MOTHER. They can't hear you? Why, what's the matter with the cattle?

OLD PIPES. Ah. There's nothing the matter with the cattle. It's with me and my pipes that something is the matter. (*He looks at his pouch.*) I do not earn my wages. I shall go straight down to the village and give back this money.

MOTHER. Nonsense! You've piped as well as you could. Who could expect anything more? And what would we do without the money?

OLD PIPES. I don't know. But I'm going down now to pay it back.

MOTHER. Not tonight you aren't.

OLD PIPES. I could not sleep tonight with money I know now I do not deserve.

MOTHER. But the sun has set.

OLD PIPES. The moon is bright. (*He starts slowly down the hill.*)

MOTHER (*calling after him*). You always were a stubborn child! (*She goes into the cottage and slams the door.*)

> (*The moonlight brightens the path.* OLD PIPES *sits to rest, leaning against the oak tree. All is quiet. Then there is a knocking from inside the tree.* OLD PIPES *rises and looks at the tree in wonder.*)

DRYAD (*inside tree*). Let me out! Please let me out!

OLD PIPES. This must be a dryad tree! I've always wanted to see a dryad. I'll let her out, if I can find the key. (*He examines the tree as the* DRYAD *continues to call.*) Now here is a strange piece of bark. Like the handle of a key. I'll try it. (*He turns the piece of bark. The tree trunk opens and a beautiful* DRYAD *stands in the opening.*)

DRYAD (*stepping quickly out of the tree and standing gazing*). Oh, lovely! Lovely! How long it is since I have seen anything like this! And how good of you to let me out! I am so happy and so thankful that I must kiss you, you dear old man! (*She stands on tiptoe and kisses him on* BOTH *cheeks.*) You don't know how doleful it is to be shut up so long in a tree. I don't mind in the winter, for then I am glad to be sheltered; but in summer it is a rueful thing not to be able to see all the beauties of the world. And it's ever so long since I've been let out. When people come at the right time, they either don't hear me, or they are frightened and run away. But you, you dear old man, were not frightened, and you looked for the key, and you have let me out. Now I shall not go back until winter has come and the air has grown cold. Oh, it is glorious! What can I do to show you how grateful I am?

OLD PIPES. I am very glad that I let you out, since I see it makes you so happy. But I must admit that I tried to find the key because I had a great desire to see a dryad. But if you wish to do something for me, you can; if you happen to be going down toward the village.

DRYAD. I will go anywhere for you.

OLD PIPES. Well, then, I wish you would take this little bag of money to the Mayor and tell him that Old Pipes cannot receive pay for services which he does not perform. It is now some time since I have been able to make the cattle hear me, when I pipe to call them home. I did not know this until tonight, but now that I do know it I cannot keep the money. (*He hands her the pouch.*) Thank you and good night.

DRYAD. Good night. And thank you over and over and over and over.

(OLD PIPES *starts up the hill. The* DRYAD *turns toward the village. Then she stops and looks after* OLD PIPES. *She darts behind the tree, peeping out to watch him.*)

OLD PIPES. (*he is twenty years younger now; but he does not know it.*) To be sure this path does not seem at all steep, and I can walk along it quite easily. But it would have tired me dreadfully to come up all the way from the village. (*He chuckles.*) I'll not tell Mother about that dryad; she'd be sure to disapprove!

MOTHER (*coming onto the porch and peering at him*). Is it you, son? Are you already back? What did the Mayor say? Did he take the money?

OLD PIPES (*shouting*). I met a person who took it to the village for me and saved me the trip.

MOTHER. How do you know that the person will take it to the Mayor? You will lose it, and the villagers will never get it. Oh, Pipes! Pipes! When will you be old enough to have ordinary common sense?

OLD PIPES. I haven't a doubt that the money will be delivered safely.

MOTHER. Well, I'VE plenty of doubts. But you've had nothing to eat and I'll get it now, though where we're ever to get another penny to keep body and soul together, I DON'T know! (*She grumbles into the cottage.*)

OLD PIPES (*sits in the moonlight on the edge of the porch*). When will I be old enough to have ordinary common sense? Dear Mother, since I'm so very old I hardly expect to grow any wiser. (*He yawns and nods and sleeps.*)

DRYAD (*coming out from behind the tree*). That is a good and honest old man, and it is a shame that he should lose this money. I don't believe the people in the village would take it from one who has served them so long. Often I've heard the sweet notes of his pipes. I'm going to give the money back to him. (*She quickly runs up the path, slips the pouch into* OLD PIPES's *pocket, and silently speeds away.*)

(*The lights dim to off.*

When the lights come up again, it is the next afternoon. OLD PIPES *is walking up the hill. He has an axe over his shoulder and he is whistling as he strides along.*)

MOTHER (*coming onto porch*). Why are you coming home in the dark? And where have you been all day?

OLD PIPES (*shouting*). It isn't dark yet, Mother. I've been cutting wood. Tomorrow I'll bring us a fine stack of it.

MOTHER. You needn't try at your age to make up for losing your piping wages by wood chopping!

OLD PIPES. I've not felt so well in years, Mother. I don't know what's happened to me. Maybe it's just the beautiful summer air.

MOTHER. You're just going to wear yourself out and get sick, that's what! (*She goes in.*)

OLD PIPES. (*He puts his hand in his coat pocket and draws out the pouch.*) Why how did THIS get there? Oh, I am stupid! I really thought that I had seen a dryad! When I sat down by the big tree, I must have gone to sleep and dreamed it all. I came home thinking I'd given the money to a dryad, when it was in my pocket all the time. I'll take it to the Mayor tonight. But first I must play my pipes. (*He goes into the cottage and comes back with his pipes. He sits on the porch and starts to finger the pipes.*)

MOTHER (*calling from the cottage*). Now what are you going to do? If you will not consent to be paid, why are you going to pipe?

OLD PIPES. I shall pipe for my own pleasure. It is the time of day when I must always pipe, whether the cattle hear me or not.

(*He pipes loud and clear. At the first notes the sleeping* PIPES ECHO-DWARF *on the ledge stirs and wonders. Then he jumps up angrily and echoes the pipes.*)

OLD PIPES (*stopping short*). Aha! What has happened to my pipes? They must have been clogged up of late, but now they are as clear and good as ever. And listen to that fine echo they make! (*He plays again and the* ECHO-DWARF *angrily answers.*)

(MARIE *and* MARTIN *run on stage from the Village down right.*)

MARIE. Why, who can be blowing those pipes?

(*The pipes stop and, after a moment, there is a distant sound of tinkling bells, with echoes.*)

MARTIN. The cattle are starting down! We don't need to go for them! Let's go tell everyone! (*They rush off down right.*)

(*The angry* PIPES ECHO-DWARF *stamps his feet and disappears behind the mountain.*)

OLD PIPES (*putting down his pipes and rising*). It's wonderful to have my pipes sound so clear and good. I can't understand it. I'll go now and return the money. Somehow I don't feel tired at all this evening. (*He starts down the hill. When he reaches the oak tree, he stops and looks at it.*) Funny about that dream I had about a dryad!

DRYAD (*appearing from behind the tree*). Good evening, my dear friend!

OLD PIPES. Oh, ho! Is it really you? I thought my seeing you was only a dream!

DRYAD. A dream! If you only knew how happy you have made me, you would not think it a dream. And do you not feel happier too? You play so beautifully on your pipes now that you are twenty years younger!

OLD PIPES. Twenty years younger??

DRYAD (*laughing*). Two kisses from a dryad, you know.

OLD PIPES (*rubbing one cheek and then the other*). Two kisses from you yesterday. (*laughs*) No wonder I could cut the wood today. I didn't understand it. I have really grown younger. I thank you, good Dryad. It was the finding of the money in my pocket that made me think it was a dream.

DRYAD. I put it there when you were asleep, because I thought you should keep it. Good-by, kind honest man. May you live long and be as happy as I am now. (*She disappears off up left.*)

OLD PIPES. Twenty years younger and I can blow my pipes as I used to. But still I must return the money which I have not earned. (*He goes on down the hill, walking happily, and off to the village.*)

(*From up left there is the sound of an angry little voice.*)

PIPES ECHO-DWARF (*off*). No, no, no! Don't try to stop me! I'm going to find out about this! (*He enters with three other DWARFS tugging at him.*)

FIDDLER ECHO-DWARF. Why are you so angry?

CHILDREN'S SHOUTS ECHO-DWARF. You mustn't leave the mountain!

SINGER ECHO-DWARF. You must stay and do your job!

PIPES ECHO-DWARF (*stamping his feet*). I won't stand for it!

FIDDLER ECHO-DWARF. STAND for it? You've grown so fat and lazy you can hardly STAND at all!

PIPES ECHO-DWARF. It isn't fair!

CHILDREN'S SHOUTS ECHO-DWARF. Why isn't it fair? You've had a long vacation!

SINGER ECHO-DWARF. And it's only once a day for you!

PIPES ECHO-DWARF. I've been deceived! I thought I had retired!

FIDDLER ECHO-DWARF (*mimicking as an echo*). Tired . . . tired . . . tired. (*The other ECHO-DWARFS join in and make a taunting little soft chorus.*)

SINGER ECHO-DWARF. What are you going to do about it?

PIPES ECHO-DWARF. I'm going to find that old man and see what's up. Maybe it's just an accident and won't happen again.

CHILDREN'S SHOUTS ECHO-DWARF. You'd better stay and do your job. You're the only Pipes Echo, you know.

PIPES ECHO-DWARF. That I know. None of YOU could do it!

CHILDREN'S SHOUTS ECHO-DWARF. None of us wants to do it. I love my job, even though it's a busy one to echo the children's voices. (*He softly echoes children's shouts.*)

SINGER ECHO-DWARF. And no one could have more fun than I as the singer echo. (*He softly echoes a song.*)

FIDDLER ECHO-DWARF. Except me! To fiddle is the most fun. (*He echoes a tune.*)

PIPES ECHO-DWARF. But I've done my job, and it's not fair to make me work again. (*He pulls away from the others and stamps off down the hill. The other* ECHO-DWARFS *run off up left and go back of the mountain.*)

(*The* DRYAD *appears from behind her tree. She is dancing and humming.*)

PIPES ECHO-DWARF (*meeting her*). What are YOU doing here? How did you get out of your tree?

DRYAD. Doing? I am being happy, that's what I am doing. I was let out of my tree by the good old man who plays the pipes to call the cattle down from the mountain, and it makes me happier because I have been of service to him. I gave him two kisses, and now he is young enough to play his pipes as well as ever.

PIPES ECHO-DWARF (*very angrily*). You are the cause of this great evil that has come upon me! You are the wicked creature who has started this old man pipe-playing again!

What have I ever done to you that you should make me work again to echo those wretched pipes?

DRYAD (*laughing*). What a funny little fellow you are! All you have to do is echo once a day the merry notes of Old Pipes. Fie upon you! You are lazy and selfish. You should rejoice at the good fortune of the old man. Go home and learn to be fair and generous, and you may then be happy!

PIPES ECHO-DWARF (*lunging at her*). Insolent creature! (*She darts behind the tree.*) Come back here! (*He waddles after her, shaking his fist.*) I'll make you suffer for this!

(*The DRYAD runs lightly up the hill and off left.*)

PIPES ECHO-DWARF. (*He has stamped around the tree and now he sits with his head in his hands.*) I'll think of some trick to pay you back! I'll get her back in her tree and break off the key, so no one can ever let her out again!

(OLD PIPES *enters from village, followed by* MARIE *and* MARTIN.)

MARIE. We don't need to help you up the hill today, Old Pipes.

MARTIN. Are you really and truly twenty years younger?

OLD PIPES. It's a miracle, that's what it is. But be careful YOU don't get kissed by a dryad.

MARIE. We'll be careful all right. We'd just disappear into wherever we came from. Ten years a kiss!

OLD PIPES. And what will you do for the rest of the summer, since I've taken your job away from you?

MARTIN. What will we do? Oho, what we WILL do!

MARIE (*laughing*). That's never a problem.

MARTIN. And we can go to the mountain meadows whenever we want anyway.

MARIE. But not have to go if we'd rather do something else.

MARTIN. It's more fun to do ANYTHING if you don't HAVE to.

OLD PIPES. Well, perhaps. But the best thing is to HAVE to do the thing in all the world you WANT MOST to do. Like me! Come up the hill when you don't HAVE to and visit me when you WANT to.

MARTIN. We will. Good-by, Old Pipes.

MARIE. We certainly will! Good-by, Old Pipes.

OLD PIPES. Good-by. And tell your father again that he really should have taken back the money that I didn't earn.

MARIE. Father and everyone else is so happy to hear your wonderful pipes again.

MARTIN. What did he say. . . . "It is a great wonder, it is a great wonder. . . ."

MARIE. ". . . and I refuse cate-gor-i-cally to take back the money!!" Good-by. (*The children wave to him as he strides off up the hill.*)

MARTIN. Twenty years. Whew! Imagine! (*They go off right.*)

(OLD PIPES *is now near the oak tree. He stops to look at it, and sees the little* DWARF.)

OLD PIPES. Hello. I didn't see you at first. I was looking for my dryad. Have you seen a dryad?

PIPES ECHO-DWARF. I'm looking for her too. What do you want with her?

OLD PIPES. She has done me such a great service. But there is one more thing I wonder if she would do for me.

PIPES ECHO-DWARF. I think she's done QUITE enough.

OLD PIPES. When I was so old myself I didn't notice how very old my mother was; but now it shocks me to see how feeble she is. I shall ask the Dryad to make my Mother younger too.

PIPES ECHO-DWARF (*grinning*). Your idea is a good one! But a dryad can make no person younger but one who lets her out of her tree.

OLD PIPES. Is that true? I didn't know that. It is a problem.

PIPES ECHO-DWARF. No problem at all. Tell the Dryad what you want, and ask her to step into her tree for a short time. Then bring your mother to open the tree and the Dryad will kiss her.

OLD PIPES. Excellent! I will go instantly and search for the Dryad.

PIPES ECHO-DWARF. I'm glad you like my plan, but you needn't say anything to her about my suggesting it. I'm willing that you should have all the credit for the idea. (*From off up left the* DRYAD *is singing.*) Here she comes now. Good luck to you!

OLD PIPES. Thank you, my little friend.

(PIPES ECHO-DWARF *slinks behind the tree, as the* DRYAD *runs down the hill.*)

DRYAD. My dear good man. I'm so happy. I hope you are happy too. I've been wondering if there is ANYthing else I can do for you; for you who have given me my glorious freedom.

OLD PIPES. Dear Dryad, you have made me twenty years younger. If you would kiss my old mother twice, then she would be the right age for me RELATIVELY!

DRYAD. I had already thought of that, and several times I have waited about your cottage, hoping to meet your mother; but she seldom comes out, and you know a dryad cannot enter a house.

OLD PIPES. But I thought you could only work your magic on a person who let you out of a tree. I thought I might ask you to go into your tree and have my mother let you out.

DRYAD. I should dreadfully dislike to go back in my tree. And it is not at all necessary. I can make your mother younger at any time she will give me the opportunity.

OLD PIPES. Then I wasn't told the truth.

DRYAD. Told the truth by whom? Who put this idea into your head?

OLD PIPES. A little dwarf whom I met here in the woods.

DRYAD. Oh! I see it all. It is the scheme of the awful Echo-Dwarf, your enemy and mine. But he really doesn't know anything about my magic! Where is he?

OLD PIPES. He has gone away.

DRYAD. (*She spies the* DWARF *as he sneaks from behind the tree and tries to run off down the hill.*) There he is! Seize him! (OLD PIPES *catches the* DWARF *by a leg. The* DRYAD *opens the tree.*) Now, stick him in there, and we will shut him up! (OLD PIPES *puts the struggling* DWARF *into the tree and the* DRYAD *pushes the tree shut.*) There! Now we need not be afraid of him. And I shall be very glad to make your mother younger. Will you ask her to come out and meet me?

OLD PIPES. I will practice a bit on my pipes, and I will ask her to come out and listen.

DRYAD. I will be there when you need me. (*She runs off up left.*)

OLD PIPES. (*He walks up the hill to his cottage and calls eagerly.*) Mother! Mother! Please bring me my pipes.

MOTHER (*coming out on porch with the pipes*). About time! About time! Here they are. And you too worn out with traipsing to the village to be able to blow them!

OLD PIPES. Mother, don't you see I'm not worn out at all. I'm not even tired. And I'll tell you why. I've been kissed twice by a dryad and I'm twenty years younger; that's why!

MOTHER. Stuff and nonsense! Kissed by a dryad indeed! Poppy-cock! There are no such things, and if there are they are evil and I'll have nothing to do with them.

OLD PIPES. But Mother, she will make you younger too.

MOTHER. You ought to be ashamed of yourself, if you did let yourself be kissed by any such creature—which I doubt. I don't believe a word of it. Anyone feels better sometimes than others. Never mention a dryad to me again! (*She storms off into the house and slams the door.*)

OLD PIPES. (*He sits sadly and plays his pipes. The muffled echo comes from inside the oak tree.* OLD PIPES *listens to the echo and smiles. Then he rises and shouts.*) Mother! I'm off now to catch a fish for our supper! (*He goes off up left.*)

MOTHER (*comes out on the porch and sits wearily on the edge of it*). He's gone off to catch a fish. Ah me! I won't let him know that I'm so tired I don't know whether or not I have strength enough to cook the fish. Alas! I have grown so old and so blind and so deaf that I am utterly useless. (*She nods and sleeps.*)

(*As soon as the* MOTHER *is sleeping, the* DRYAD *instantly appears. Softly the* DRYAD *kisses the* MOTHER *on each cheek, then disappears.*)

MOTHER (*jerking awake*). Goodness me, I must have dozed off! My son will be here and I'm not ready for him! (*She rises quickly.*) It is astonishing how much better I feel. How a little sleep does refresh one! (*She bustles happily into the cottage.*)

(*The lights fade out.*
    There is a sound of wind blowing. The lights come up gradually and the DRYAD *runs on from up left. She is shivering and hugging herself. She runs to the oak tree and opens it.*)

DRYAD. Come out, Echo-Dwarf! Winter is coming, and I want the comfortable shelter of my tree for myself. Today the cattle will come down from the mountain for the last time this year; they will stay for the winter near the village and their barns. The pipes will no longer sound, and you can go to your mountain and have a holiday until next spring.

PIPES ECHO-DWARF (*stumbling out of the tree, blinking*). I just may break off that key and you will never get out again! I just MAY!

DRYAD. No, no, you won't. You have learned your lesson! Haven't you, haven't you? Tell me you have!

PIPES ECHO-DWARF. I thought I'd have to sit in that old musty tree forever! Yes, yes, I HAVE learned my lesson! Cross my heart, I have!

DRYAD. And I'll tell you a secret! My kiss is magic for anyone, even if he doesn't let me out of the tree; and ALSO it does not matter really if you break off the key. Another will grow next spring. I know my good piper will come and let me out again when the warm days arrive.

PIPES ECHO-DWARF. Well, I'll be a monkey's uncle! Yes, yes, I have. I've learned my lesson. And I'll never be lazy never, ever, never, ever. . . . (*He skips off to his mountain, but turns back to say*) Well, almost never. . . .

(*The* DRYAD *stands in the opening of the tree. She is about to close her door, but she looks toward* OLD PIPES's *cottage and then runs shivering to hide at the side of the porch.* OLD PIPES *and his* MOTHER *come out on the porch. He is carrying his pipes. They sit on the edge of the porch.*)

OLD PIPES. The air is fresh and chill, Mother. The end of summer. My last piping of the year for the cattle.

MOTHER. I shall miss the tinkling of the cattle bells.

OLD PIPES. Until next spring, then! (*He plays loudly and clearly. Over the mountain peak, the* PIPES ECHO-DWARF *echoes the piping.*)

MOTHER. That was a lovely piping, and the echo has never been so beautiful!

(*The cowbells tinkle in the distance, with their little echo.* OLD PIPES *and his* MOTHER *listen contentedly. The* DRYAD *moves quietly and kisses* OLD PIPES *on his cheek; then she kisses the* MOTHER. *The* DRYAD *then runs quickly and quietly to her tree and stands in its doorway.*)

MOTHER. Did you kiss me, son? Thank you.

OLD PIPES (*touching his cheek*). I think, Mother, we get younger and younger.

MOTHER. Oh you! You've never known the difference between what's truth and what's fancy!

(*The bells are still tinkling as the* FIDDLER *leads the village* CHILDREN *on stage down right. As he fiddles, the* CHILDREN *sing and dance. From the mountain, all of the* ECHO DWARFS *stick up their heads and echo the gay sounds. As the lights fade, the* FIDDLER *leads the* CHILDREN *back into the village.* OLD PIPES *and his* MOTHER *rise and go off into their cottage. The* ECHO DWARFS *disappear behind their mountain. The* DRYAD *in her tree closes her door.*)

PRODUCTION NOTES

The ideal place for this play is outdoors in a spot where there is a sharp hillside, with bushes or rocks for the Echo-Dwarfs and a tree for the Dryad. Put some real bushes at the side of the tree; the Dryad pretends to come from inside the tree, but actually comes from behind it. Of course, if you have a real tree that is hollow, you are in luck. I know one—a giant redwood that was hollowed out by fire many hundreds of years ago. Lucky children have acted many plays near that tree.

Do not combine artificial scenery with outdoor scenery. A cutout of mountains would look completely wrong when everything else is real. The only made scenery should be the porch of the cottage. The rest of the cottage would be imagined to be behind trees or hedge or rocks or bushes—whatever you have.

For an indoor production, the scenery is simple and is never changed. Against a blue sky backdrop on which the base of a big mountain is sketched, place some screens which are covered with cutouts of lower crags of the mountain. Leave room behind the screens for ladders and high stools, so the dwarfs can stand there and stick their heads over the crags. To make the ledge for the sleeping dwarf, nail a board between the tops of two step-ladders; he can climb up and down the ladders behind the screens to get to and from his ledge.

Downstage right is the clearing outside the pretend village. This is the stage floor with a few low bushes, and a rock for the Fiddler to sit on. Put a platform at stage center and stand the Dryad's tree on it. At the left of this platform, place another platform on blocks of wood, so that it will be higher than the first; and place a third platform to the left of that one, on higher blocks. On the left end of this platform set a low table for the porch of the cottage. Cover the exit into the pretend cottage with some cardboard cutouts of pine trees. Nail cardboard cutouts of rocks and bushes to the front edge of these three platforms; the cutouts gradually get taller as they cover the rising slant of the platforms. The acting of the characters who

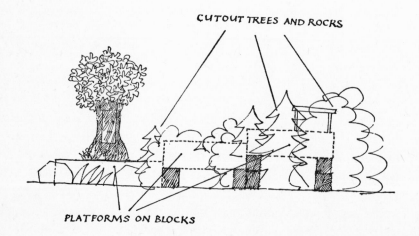

CUTOUT TREES AND ROCKS

PLATFORMS ON BLOCKS

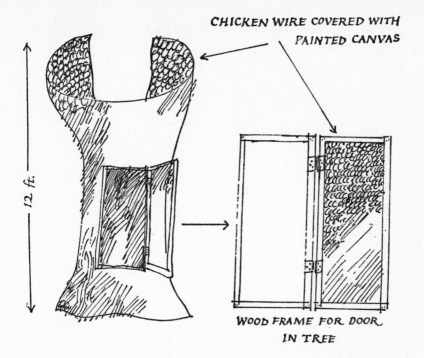

CHICKEN WIRE COVERED WITH
PAINTED CANVAS

12 ft.

WOOD FRAME FOR DOOR
IN TREE

climb or descend this hill will make the audience know it is a
steep climb!

To make the tree, use a big roll of chicken wire with an
opening cut out of the front of it and framed with wood for the
doorway. Cover the wire with brown cloth painted to look like
bark. Stand this tree on the first platform and brace it securely
from the back. For the door, make a cardboard or wooden flap to
match the tree trunk and hinge this door to the wooden frame
of the tree's opening. Flank the tree with cardboard cutouts of
low bushes to cover the bracings.

You will find excellent ideas for costumes in any illustrated
edition of Johanna Spyri's *Heidi*. Old Pipes might indeed look
very much like Heidi's grandfather. He wears knee breeches, a
blouse, a short jacket, high socks, sturdy boots, and a big flat hat
to which a long beard is attached. The Fiddler is dressed much
the same way, except he wears shoes with buckles, and a
pointed hat with a feather. The village girls have full skirts with
puffy petticoats, blouses and boleros. The boys wear blouses,
short pants like lederhosen, with suspenders; some have felt

hats with feathers. Old Pipes's Mother wears a long full skirt a long-sleeved blouse, an apron, a shawl, wire spectacles, and a little cap which has white cotton hair sewn to it. The Echo Dwarfs' blouses and bloomers are of woodsy dark greens and browns. They have pointed soft slippers, pointed caps to which are stapled big pointed ears, and little pointed beards. The Dryad is a lovely sprite who wears green tights and leotard under a filmy green wisp of material fastened only at the shoulders. On her loose hair is a garland of leaves. She is barefooted, or wears soft slippers. All of her movements are a dancer's.

There are very few props in this play. The Fiddler naturally needs a fiddle. If he cannot really play it, he should practice his pretend playing so that it looks completely real. Offstage a musician can do the real playing, or you can use violin records.

Old Pipes can play a recorder, or he can pretend to play pipes which can be made of cardboard to look like Panpipes or to look like Alpine pipes. Offstage use a musician with a recorder or flute; or use recordings. Old Pipes should have a gnarled walking stick, a leather pouch with coins in it to jingle, and an axe.

PAN PIPES.   ALPINE
PIPES

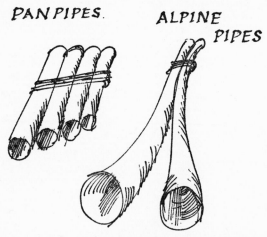

One of the most important members of your crew is not on stage. He has charge of the sounds. He may be the one who plays the records of the fiddle and pipes music and he will know the music cues perfectly and be able to follow the script exactly. He will have charge of the door slams. He will jingle the cow bells at the appropriate times and with the appropriate dynamics.

The Dwarfs will need lots of practice, so that they can reproduce vocally the endings of their own special stage sounds. They might try covering their mouths with their hands and turning their heads to get effects of distance. They must be very alert and must time their echoes precisely. The villagers must be sure not to look at the Dwarfs. To them the echoes are familiar sounds.

Old Pipes and his Mother will show their changing ages by convincing characterization in their gestures, walks, attitudes and voices. It is unnecessary to use much make-up—it is unconvincing on young faces; good acting will make you the age you need to be!

A good way to try out for these parts is to have everyone pantomime walking, standing, sitting as he thinks an old person would. The ones who act old age best will be the ones who *think* old age best.

Folk tunes from Switzerland are good ones to use for the Fiddler's songs. Two gay and familiar ones are "Weggis Song" and "Vreneli."

It would be exciting to put the entire play to a musical score. If you listen to a recording of Prokofieff's *Peter and the Wolf*, you will get good ideas about how this might be done. Here is a fine project for drama, music and dance. Do you have a music teacher who might help you compose music to fit the action, mood and characters of this play? If any of you ever do this, please let me know what you did and how it worked!

CHOP-CHIN AND THE GOLDEN DRAGON

CHOP-CHIN AND THE GOLDEN DRAGON

Dramatized from a story by Laura E. Richards
in *Toto's Merry Winter*.
Little, Brown and Company, Boston, 1887.

CHARACTERS

CHOP-CHIN, TEN-YEAR-OLD SON OF
LY-CHEE, SWEEPER OF THE IMPERIAL COURTYARD
THREE OTHER SWEEPERS
HIS CELESTIAL MAJESTY WAH-SONG
THE PRINCELY PARASOL-HOLDER
THE UNIQUE UMBRELLA-OPENER
THE CELESTIAL TRAIN-HOLDERS
SENTINEL OF THE IMPERIAL COURTYARD
THE CHIEF PILLOW-THUMPER
THE TIER OF THE STRINGS OF THE CELESTIAL NIGHTCAP
THE PRINCIPAL POURER OF WINE
THE FINISHING-TOUCHER
FOUR GUARDS OF THE BRONZE GATE OF THE SHRINE OF THE
    GOLDEN DRAGON
FOUR GUARDS OF THE STEEL GATE
FOUR GUARDS OF THE IVORY GATE
FOUR PRIESTS OF THE GOLDEN GATE
PROPERTY MAN
ORCHESTRA

The stage is bare, except for benches upstage right for the ORCHESTRA *and a table and stool down left for the* PROPERTY MAN.

The PROPERTY MAN *enters, carrying a tall frame with imperial insignia on it. This is the gate to the palace courtyard. He places the frame upstage center, observes its position, straightens it a bit, shrugs, and exits. He returns with four buckets and four brooms. He places these near his table down left and then sits impassively on his stool.*

The members of the ORCHESTRA *enter, carrying their instruments. They come center, bow to the audience, and go to sit on their benches up right. Their leader strikes his gong.* ORCHESTRA *sits up straight and starts to play.*

As the music continues, the SWEEPERS *enter right. They are barefooted and carry their scrubbing shoes. At stage center they bow to the audience and then sit on the floor and put on their scrubbing shoes. The music stops.*

FIRST SWEEPER. The marble pavement must be as clean as the sky after rain, and as white as the breath of the frost.

SECOND SWEEPER. In case His Celestial Majesty desires to taste the freshness of the air today.

THIRD SWEEPER. For this high duty I wear out two pairs of scrubbing shoes in a month.

LY-CHEE. My little Chop-Chin in two years will be old enough to engage with us in this great and honored privilege.

FIRST SWEEPER. He is a good son to you.

SECOND SWEEPER. Each day he brings your dinner.

THIRD SWEEPER. And watches us admiringly.

LY-CHEE. He is a good son, and is my joy. I have been both father and mother to him for many years.

(ORCHESTRA *plays.* SWEEPERS *rise. Each gets broom and bucket from* PROPERTY MAN. FIRST SWEEPER *goes upstage right, tosses imaginary water straight at audience, puts bucket down, dances vigorously as he scrubs and sweeps.* SECOND SWEEPER *takes his bucket up left, tosses imaginary water in a swooping circle.* THIRD SWEEPER *takes his bucket down right, tosses imaginary water through his spread legs. They are very gay and make a dancing game of their work.* LY-CHEE *takes his bucket down center stage, facing the audience.* At this moment from upstage left the SENTINEL *of the Imperial Courtyard enters, followed by* HIS CELESTIAL MAJESTRY, *the* CELESTIAL TRAIN-HOLDERS, *the* PRINCELY PARASOL-HOLDER *and the* UNIQUE UMBRELLA-OPENER. FIRST, SECOND *and* THIRD SWEEPERS *stop dancing and bow to the floor.* SENTINEL *comes through the gate and stands at one side of it. At the very moment* HIS MAJESTY *is in the gateway,* LY-CHEE, *who has been winking at the audience and thinking up an exciting way to do his job, tosses the imaginary water from his bucket BACKWARDS with a flourish. Everyone shrieks.* LY-CHEE *turns, sees the calamity, falls flat on his face. Music stops.)*

CELESTIAL MAJESTY *(after a moment's dreadful pause)*. Princely Parasol-Holder, our feet are wet. (PARASOL-HOLDER *groans and chatters his teeth in anguish.)* Unique Umbrella-Opener, our petticoat is completely saturated. (UMBRELLA-OPENER *tears at his clothing, shakes his head wildly, moans in agony.)* Let this man's head be removed at sunrise tomorrow! *(shriek from the* SWEEPERS)

FIRST SWEEPER *(flat on the floor, face down)*. Have mercy, Celestial Majesty. Spare Ly-Chee who has given you long and faithful service.

SECOND SWEEPER *(in the same position)*. Have mercy, Celestial Majesty. Spare Ly-Chee who has lived an upright and devout life.

THIRD SWEEPER *(in the same position)*. Have mercy, Celestial Majesty. Spare Ly-Chee whose little son looks to him for his daily sustenance.

CELESTIAL MAJESTY. Our feet are wet. Our petticoat is saturated. Let this man's head be removed at sunrise tomorrow.

UNIQUE UMBRELLA-HOLDER *(bowing to the floor)*. O Celestial Majesty, who can do no wrong, I have known long this faithful sweeper and know he is afflicted in his hearing and did not hear the coming of your Celestial Majesty and I intercede. . . .

CELESTIAL MAJESTY (*enraged*). Are our clothes to be changed, or do we stand here all day in wetness? We swear that unless the Golden Dragon himself come down from his altar and beg for this man's life, this man shall die!

> (CELESTIAL MAJESTY *signals to the* SENTINEL, *who goes to* LY-CHEE. CELESTIAL MAJESTY *circles the stage with his followers in order to get his train turned around, goes back through the gate and off up left.* SENTINEL *raises* LY-CHEE *from the floor, as* ORCHESTRA *plays.* LY-CHEE *removes his scrubbing shoes and goes with the* SENTINEL *through the gate and off up left.* PROPERTY MAN *with a shrug gets* LY-CHEE's *shoes, bucket and broom, and takes them back to table and sits.* SWEEPERS *rise and cluster together upstage left. They whisper and gesture wildly in fear and excitement.*
>
> CHOP-CHIN *enters down right. On his head is a bowl of rice. He carries a melon. He stops and looks around. Music stops.* SWEEPERS *see him and are silent. Then they file toward him solemnly, holding out their hands, palms down.*)

FIRST SWEEPER. What is man's life but a string of beads, which at one time or another must be broken?

CHOP-CHIN. What words are these? Why do you look and speak so strangely? Where is my father?

SWEEPERS. Alas!

SECOND SWEEPER. Your father will wear out no more scrubbing shoes.

THIRD SWEEPER. It chanced through some evil fate that at the very moment His Celestial Majesty stepped out into the courtyard, Ly-Chee cast a great bucketful of ice-cold water backwards, with fatal force and precision.

(CHOP-CHIN *shudders, puts down his bowl and melon, and hides his face in his hands.*)

FIRST SWEEPER. Picture to yourself the dreadful scene! The Celestial Petticoat of yellow satin damask was drenched. The Celestial Shoes of chicken-skin embroidered in gold were ruined.

SECOND SWEEPER. We fell to the ground and cried aloud and besought the Celestial Mercy for our comrade.

THIRD SWEEPER. The Unique Umbrella-Opener tore his clothes, and shook his hair wildly about his face, with moans of agony.

FIRST SWEEPER. The Princely Parasol-Holder, who is a kindly man, also made intercession.

SECOND SWEEPER. The Celestial Train-Holders silently shook with sorrow.

THIRD SWEEPER. But the Emperor swore that unless the Golden Dragon himself begs for Ly-Chee's life, he will die at sunrise.

(CHOP-CHIN *kisses the hands of the* SWEEPERS, *picks up his bowl and melon, and slowly walks offstage left.* ORCHESTRA *plays.*

The SWEEPERS *sit down, take off their shoes, rise, bow to the audience, and go off right. The* PROPERTY MAN *picks up the buckets and brooms and takes them offstage. The* ORCHESTRA *members get up, stretch and relax; some whisper together, some sit down again and sleep, some eat food they have brought with them. It is the end of the scene.*

PROPERTY MAN *removes* PALACE GATE, *takes it offstage, and returns with a high table with a box fastened to the top of it. He has a large cloth of gold over his arm. He places the table upstage center and spreads the gold cloth over the box and table. He ambles offstage and returns with the Golden Dragon. He places this on top of the box, and then goes back to his table and sits. Orchestra leader sounds the gong.* ORCHESTRA *assembles and starts to play.*

FOUR PRIESTS, *in robes of gold, enter. They carry golden censers. They come center, bow to the audience, and then walk upstage and stand in a line in front of the altar, facing audience.* FOUR IVORY GUARDS, *in white armor, enter. They carry pikes. They bow to audience and then stand in a row a few feet in front of the* PRIESTS. FOUR STEEL GUARDS, *in steel armor, enter. They carry pikes. They bow to audience and then stand in a row a few feet in front of the* IVORY GUARDS. FOUR BRONZE GUARDS *in bronze armor, enter with their pikes. They bow to audience and then stand in a row a few feet in front of the* STEEL GUARDS.

CHOP-CHIN *enters from down left. He wears a white tunic with a wide crimson sash. He carries high above his head a brass bowl. He walks solemnly to stage center below the array of* GUARDS. *Music stops. Facing the* BRONZE GUARDS, CHOP-CHIN *holds the bowl in his left hand, and knocks on the air three times with his right hand. The* PROPERTY MAN *knocks on his table for the sound. The* BRONZE GUARDS *point their pikes at* CHOP-CHIN.)

BRONZE GUARDS. What seekest thou in the court of the Holy Dragon?

CHOP-CHIN. The powerful Prince Tong-Ki-Tcheng lies sick of a fever. He sends you greeting and a draught of cool wine. He begs your prayers to the Holy Dragon that he may recover from his grievous sickness, and prays that I may pass onward to the shrine.

(*Each* GUARD *drinks from the brass bowl.*)

BRONZE GUARDS. Our prayers for Tong-Ki-Tcheng shall go up without ceasing. Pass on, fair youth, and good success go with thee!

(*Two of the* BRONZE GUARDS *move sideways to stage right as the other two move sideways to stage left.* ORCHESTRA *plays.* CHOP-CHIN *steps upstage and knocks again. He now faces the* STEEL GUARDS *with their fixed pikes.*)

STEEL GUARDS. What seekest thou in the court of the Holy Dragon?

CHOP-CHIN. Tong-Ki-Tcheng sends you greeting, and a draught of cool wine. He begs your prayers to the Holy Dragon that he may recover from his grievous sickness, and prays that I may pass onward to the shrine.

(*Each* GUARD *drinks from the brass bowl.*)

STEEL GUARDS. Our prayers for Tong-Ki-Tcheng shall go up without ceasing. Pass on, fair youth, and good success go with thee!

(*Two of the* STEEL GUARDS *step sideways to either side of the stage, but not so far as the* BRONZE GUARDS, *as* ORCHESTRA *plays.* CHOP-CHIN *advances upstage and faces the* IVORY GUARDS. *He knocks.*)

IVORY GUARDS. What seekest thou in the court of the Holy Dragon?

CHOP-CHIN. Tong-Ki-Tcheng sends you greeting, and a draught of cool wine. He begs your prayers to the Holy Dragon that he may recover from his grievous sickness, and prays that I may pass onward to the shrine.

(*Each* GUARD *drinks from the brass bowl.*)

IVORY GUARDS. Our prayers for Tong-Ki-Tcheng shall go up without ceasing. Pass on, fair youth, and good success go with thee!

(*Two* IVORY GUARDS *step sideways to either side of the stage, but not so far as the* STEEL GUARDS, *as the* ORCHESTRA *plays.* CHOP-CHIN *is now facing the* PRIESTS OF GOLD. *He raises the bowl high.*)

CHOP-CHIN. Ka Ho Hai! Hai Nong Ti!
    Tong-Ki-Tcheng Lo Hum Ki Ni!

PRIESTS (*swinging their censers*). Rash youth! By what right or by whose order comest thou here to the Sacred Shrine of the Golden Dragon?

CHOP-CHIN (*kneeling and extending the bowl*). By the right of mortal sickness, most Holy Priests, and by order of the noble Tong-Ki-Tcheng. He prays thee to drink to his recovery from his grievous sickness, and that your prayers may go up with mine at the Golden Shrine itself.

(*Each* PRIEST *drinks from the brass bowl.*)

PRIESTS. Our prayers shall truly go up for Tong-Ki-Tcheng. We will cover thine eyes, for none save ourselves, Priests of the First Order, may look upon the face of the Holy Dragon.

(CHOP-CHIN *turns to the audience as one* PRIEST *ties a silk cloth over his eyes. Two* PRIESTS *now step to either side of* CHOP-CHIN. *The* PRIESTS *and* CHOP-CHIN *then turn to the Dragon and fall on the floor before the altar.*

There is silence, during which the BRONZE GUARDS, *then the* STEEL GUARDS, *then the* IVORY GUARDS *crumple to the floor and sleep. Then the* PRIESTS *start to snore. There is heavy breathing all over the stage.* CHOP-CHIN *lifts his head from the floor and listens. He gently touches the nearest* PRIEST; *then he rises and shakes each* PRIEST *by the shoulders. All snore in unison.*)

CHOP-CHIN. The drugged wine has done its work!

(CHOP-CHIN *gazes at the Golden Dragon. Then he straightens his shoulders and tosses his head.*)

CHOP-CHIN. For my father! For my father! (*He reaches up and lifts the Golden Dragon from the shrine. With it in his arms, he turns and looks at all the sleepers who are snoring calmly and evenly.* CHOP-CHIN *removes his crimson sash, shakes it out, and wraps the Dragon in it. Quickly he carries the Dragon past all the sleepers and off left.*

It is the end of a scene. The ORCHESTRA *members stretch, rise, and wander around the stage for exercise. The* PRIESTS *and* GUARDS *rise and saunter offstage. The* PROPERTY MAN *takes the shrine off. He brings back a bench loaded with covers and pillows. He places this bench stage center, slanted at right angle to the audience, covers the bench with a drape, places the pillows at the upstage end of the bench and folds the covers at the foot of the bench. He goes off and returns with the Courtyard Gate frame, which he sets at downstage right. Then the* PROPERTY MAN *sits at his table, the* ORCHESTRA *takes its place, the gong sounds, the music starts.*

The SENTINEL *enters right, comes center and bows, takes his position right of the gate and walks up and down.* HIS CELESTIAL MAJESTY, *in long nightgown, enters from left, followed by* CHIEF PILLOW-THUMPER. HIS MAJESTY *sits on the bed as the* PILLOW-THUMPER *thumps the pillows, bows, and stands at attention stage left.* THE TIER OF THE STRINGS OF THE CELESTIAL NIGHTCAP *enters left, kneels before* HIS MAJESTY, *rises, places cap on* HIS MAJESTY *and ties strings. Then he bows and backs stage left. The* PRINCIPAL POURER *enters with tray on which there is a wine goblet and a decanter. He bows, pours wine, offers goblet to* HIS MAJESTY, *and backs into position beside the* PILLOW-THUMPER *and the* TIER OF THE STRINGS. *Music stops.*)

CELESTIAL MAJESTY. The wine is unsavory. (*throws goblet at* POURER, *who goes onto his knees*) The nightcap is tied too loosely. (TIER *goes onto his knees*) The pillows are not thumped enough! (PILLOW-THUMPER *on his knees*) Where is the Finishing-Toucher?? (*The* FINISHING-TOUCHER *enters bowing and tucks* HIS MAJESTY *into bed.*) You are a twiddler of a Tuckerinner! (FINISHING-TOUCHER *on his knees*)

THUMPER, POURER, TIER, TOUCHER (*from their knees*). May the blessings of sweet sleep as soft as feathers fall upon your Celestial Majesty!

CELESTIAL MAJESTY. GET OUT!

(*They crawl off left backwards. The* CELESTIAL MAJESTY *folds his hands on his chest and snores. The lights dim.*

The SENTINEL *drowses in front of the gate.* CHOP-CHIN, *carrying the Dragon wrapped in the sash, enters down right.)*

SENTINEL (*straightening to attention*). What is this? Who art thou, and what monstrous burden is this thou carriest so lightly?

CHOP-CHIN. Shhh! Speak not so loud, friend! This is the Celestial Footstool!

SENTINEL. May the Holy Dragon preserve me! What has happened to it?

CHOP-CHIN. His Celestial Majesty threw it in anger at the Putter-on-of-Slippers yesterday, and broke one of its legs. All day my master, the Chief Cabinetmaker, has been at work on it, and now he has sent me with it by nightfall, that no profane eye may see clearly even the outer covering of the sacred object.

SENTINEL. Pass in. But tell me, knowest thou how it will fare with the Putter-on-of-Slippers? He is cousin to my stepfather's aunt by marriage, and I would not have ill come to so near a relative.

CHOP-CHIN. Alas, I know not! I fear it may go hard with him!

(SENTINEL *shakes his head sadly and resumes his pacing.* CHOP-CHIN *tiptoes into the bedroom, unwraps the Golden Dragon, and puts it over his head. Then he tiptoes to the foot of the bed and kneels, facing* HIS MAJESTY.)

CHOP-CHIN (*in a dreadful voice*). Wah-Song! Wah-Song! Awake!

CELESTIAL MAJESTY (*springing up in bed in terror*). Ah horror! Ah destruction! The Golden Dragon is here! (*He howls and pulls the covers over his head.*)

CHOP-CHIN. Wah-Song! Thou hast summoned me, and I am here!

CELESTIAL MAJESTY (*moaning and uncovering his face a little*). I . . . I . . . I sum . . . summon thee, most Golden and Holy Dragon?

CHOP-CHIN (*sternly*). Listen! Yesterday morning, in consequence of thine own folly in going out unannounced, thy silly shoes and petticoat became wet. For this nothing, thou has condemned to death my faithful servant Ly-Chee, who has brought me fresh melons every Tuesday for thirty years. When others interceded for his life, thou madest reply, "We swear that unless the Golden Dragon himself come down from his altar and beg for this man's life, he shall die!" (HIS MAJESTY *groans*.) Therefore, Wah-Song, I AM HERE!

CELESTIAL MAJESTY. I . . . I . . . I didn't know he brought thee melons.

CHOP-CHIN. Listen, now, to my commands. Before daybreak thou wilt send a free pardon to Ly-Chee, who now lies in prison expecting to die at sunrise.

CELESTIAL MAJESTY. I will! I will!

CHOP-CHIN. Moreover, thou wilt send him by a trusty messenger, twenty bags of gold. (HIS MAJESTY *groans*.) Furthermore, thou wilt make Ly-Chee thy Chief Sweeper for life and give him each year six brooms of gilded straw and three dozen pairs of scrubbing shoes; and his son, Chop-Chin, thou wilt appoint as Second Sweeper to help his father. Obey these orders strictly and speedily. Neglect them, even in the smallest particular, and Ha! Hum! WURRA-wurra-G-r-r-r-r!

(HIS CELESTIAL MAJESTY *falls back in terror, pillows over his head.* CHOP-CHIN *quickly takes off the dragon head, wraps it in the crimson sash again, and hurries through the gate.*)

SENTINEL. How now! What means this, boy?

CHOP-CHIN. Alas! Unhappy that I am! Was it my fault that the mended leg was a hair's-breadth shorter than the others? I must take it back to my master.

SENTINEL. Stay a moment! Thinkest thou that I might take just one peep at the Celestial Footstool? Do but lift a corner of the mantle!

CHOP-CHIN. At thy peril! Touch it not! Knowest thou not that the penalty is four hundred lashes?

SENTINEL. Pass on, then, in the name of the Dragon!

CHOP-CHIN (*bowing and hurrying away*). Good night, good sir.

> (*The* ORCHESTRA *plays.* HIS MAJESTY *gets out of bed, bows, and goes off left.* SENTINEL *bows and goes off right. Music stops.* ORCHESTRA *relaxes.* PROPERTY MAN *takes gate and bed offstage. He brings on the golden shrine and sets it upstage center, then sits on his stool. The* PRIESTS *enter, bow, and take their sleeping positions in front of shrine. The three sets of* GUARDS *do the same. The scene is now exactly the same as it was before the bedroom scene.* ORCHESTRA *begins to play.*
>
> BRONZE GUARDS *stir, stretch, and guiltily get to their feet.* STEEL GUARDS *repeat this action; then the* IVORY GUARDS. PRIESTS *begin to stir. Music stops.* PRIESTS *lift their heads and look at the shrine. They see that the Golden Dragon is gone, and they fling themselves flat on their faces and howl and moan.*)

PRIESTS (*in loud, mournful chant*). We slept! We slept! Ai! Ai! Ai! We know not why. Wow! Wow! Wow! We know not how. Because we slept the Golden Dragon hast removed itself! Because we slept, the Golden Dragon has gone away. We are desolate! Desolate! Punka-wunka-woggle! Punka-wunka-wogg!

> (*The terrified* GUARDS *fall to their knees and cover their faces.* CHOP-CHIN *tiptoes in, sets the Golden Dragon on the floor down center, pantomimes knocking, and hurries off. The* GUARDS *lift their heads at the sound of the* PROPERTY MAN'S *real knocking. The* BRONZE GUARDS *creep together*

center stage, look at the Golden Dragon, and in terror return to the sides of the stage with their backs to audience.)

BRONZE GUARDS (*on their knees, bowing and calling*). Come, come, most holy Priests of the Saki-Pan.

(*The* STEEL GUARDS *repeat this action and join the cry for the* PRIESTS. *The* IVORY GUARDS *then do the same. All the* GUARDS *are now on their knees, facing upstage, bowing and calling.*)

GUARDS. Come, come, most holy Priests of the Saki-Pan.

(PRIESTS *rise, come downstage, see the* DRAGON, *and bow before it.*)

PRIESTS. The Golden Dragon! The Golden Dragon! Glory to the Golden Dragon! (*As the* GUARDS *lie flat on the floor, the* PRIESTS *carry the Dragon back to its altar. Then the* PRIESTS *walk to the front of the stage. The* GUARDS *rise and stand at attention.*)

PRIESTS (*facing front and calling*). Glory to the Holy Dragon!

A crowd gathers down left. The GUARDS *have closed their ranks in front of the Dragon.*)

PRIESTS. Glory to the Holy Dragon! He walked abroad for the glory of his subjects. He cast upon the city the eye of blessing! Glory to the Holy Dragon, and happiness and peace to the city and to the people!

CROWD. It is for Ly-Chee! Honor to Ly-Chee! The Golden Dragon has saved him. Ly-Chee! Ly-Chee!

(LY-CHEE *and* CHOP-CHIN *enter down right, followed by the* CELESTIAL MAJESTY.)

CELESTIAL MAJESTY (*silencing the cheering crowd with a wave of his hand*). This great and good man, Ly-Chee, whom the Golden Dragon has honored, is now my Chief-Sweeper of the Courtyard. (*crowd cheers*) Let twenty bags of gold be brought to him. (*cheers*) Every year he will have six brooms of gilded straw with ivory handles and three dozen pairs of scrubbing shoes. (*cheers*) This is the will of the Golden Dragon as pronounced through me his most humble servant, the Celestial Emperor. (*cheers. The* CELESTIAL MAJESTY *turns to depart.*)

CHOP-CHIN (*shouting above the crowd*). One moment, Your Majesty! (*The noise stops. His* CELESTIAL MAJESTY *looks in amazement at* CHOP-CHIN *as does the crowd.*) Your Celestial Majesty, what is to happen to me, Chop-Chin, the son of Ly-Chee?

CELESTIAL MAJESTY (*with a puzzled look at* CHOP-CHIN). Ah, ah, yes. And his son, Chop-Chin, I now appoint as Second Sweeper to help his father.

(*The crowd cheers, as his* CELESTIAL MAJESTY *comes to the center of the stage and bows to the audience. The entire cast, in procession, comes center front, bows, exits. The* ORCHESTRA *bows and exits. The* PROPERTY MAN *takes the Golden Dragon; with it under his arm, he starts offstage. Then he turns, grins, looks all around him, and comes center and bows to the audience before he exits.*)

PRODUCTION NOTES

This play is to be produced in the style of Chinese theater tradition. There is no curtain. The scenes are indicated by stage props, which are set up by the Property Man. He wears black pajamas and black slippers. The black costume means that he is invisible to the audience. He is on the stage the entire time, except when he shuffles on and off to bring or remove props. He sits at a little table and occasionally hands a prop to an actor. He is completely disinterested in the play itself; he dozes through most of it. This actor says nothing, but he is a very important member of the cast. He must be careful not to be distracting, even though he certainly is amusing in his boredom at what is happening on stage.

The members of the Orchestra are also on the stage throughout the play and are very important to it. They too must be careful not to attract attention to themselves, when the play itself is in progress. When their leader strikes his gong, they sit up very straight and play their instruments with intense seriousness. Otherwise, they slump and nap. Chinese music sounds shrill and discordant to Western ears; the effect can be achieved by toy instruments, combs covered with tissue paper, tin pans, etc. The Orchestra members wear pajamas of a variety of colors, and slippers. Each has black hair in a single long braid. To make it, stretch a long black cotton stocking over the head, secure it at the top of the head with an elastic, and cut the rest of it into long strips to braid.

When an actor in a Chinese play enters or exits, he bows very formally to the audience; his hands are folded in front of him, and he bows from the waist.

To suggest the Chinese walk, practice taking very small running steps on tiptoe, keeping your body straight.

The language in a Chinese play is eloquent and precise. In this play many of the lines are repeated, so they will be easy to learn even though they may seem difficult at first reading.

Costumes are elaborate and are made of rich materials. Rob your attics of silk, satin, velvet draperies and old evening clothes. His Celestial Majesty is gorgeously arrayed in a long full robe with wide flowing sleeves, and a Mandarin headpiece

which has jewels and feathers on it. Attach a long sweeping beard to the headpiece. His golden slippers have upswept pointed toes. His personal attendants are almost as magnificent as he.

Even the Courtyard Sweepers are dressed beautifully, although they wear pajamas instead of robes. To make their scrubbing shoes, sew floor-mops securely to soft slippers.

The Guards at the Shrine of the Golden Dragon are magnificent. They wear pajamas of the proper color (white, steel, bronze), and breastplates, arm and leg pieces, helmets made of corrugated cardboard and sprayed with the correct matching paint.

The Priests wear long robes of golden brocade and round golden cardboard hats.

These are the props you will need:

Benches for Orchestra
Table and stool for Property Man
Frame of gate for Palace Courtyard
Instruments for Orchestra
Buckets, brooms, scrubbing shoes for Sweepers
Royal umbrella
Paper bowl for rice. Attach it to a circular base, so Chop-Chin can carry it safely on his head
Large paper melon
High table, with box attached to the top of it, for shrine
Cloth of gold to cover box and table
Golden Dragon. This is hollow, and large enough to cover Chop-Chin's head and shoulders comfortably. Make it of papier-mâché, or of chicken wire
Golden censers for the Priests. Attach gold-sprayed balls to gold cords
Pikes for the Guards. Make them of pointed broomsticks or dowels and paint them the appropriate colors
Brass bowl for wine
Silk kerchief for blindfold

Long bench with elaborate covers and pillows
Nightcap with strings for Tier
Small tray with metal or cardboard goblet and decanter

Because this play has many characters, it would be good for a classroom group. The characters, however, may be doubled up. For instance, the attendants of His Celestial Majesty in the Courtyard could be the attendants in the Royal Bedchamber. The number of Guards, Priests, Sweepers could be reduced. The Orchestra could be as few as three actors, or as many as you wish.

WITH ALL MY HEART

WITH ALL MY HEART

This little play in verse found some of its plot in
"The Three Remarks," a story by Laura E. Richards
first published in 1881 and reprinted in her book,
The Pig Brother and Other Fables and Stories,
Little, Brown and Company, Boston, 1908.

CHARACTERS

THE MINSTREL	THE COURT LADIES
THE KING	THE VILLAGERS
THE PRINCESS	THE IMPOSTOR
THE SUITORS	THE OUTLAWS
THE SHEPHERD	

(The Minstrel enters in front of the curtain, and bows to
the audience.)

MINSTREL. We will tell our tale in rhyme.
It starts with Once upon a time—
The way all fairy stories should—
A Princess beautiful and good
At her birth, as you have guessed,
Was by all lovely fairies blessed
With gracefulness and eyes so blue
And hair so gold and heart so true.
But one old dame was not invited;
She felt out-ra-ge-ous-ly slighted.
This fairy ALWAYS is the worst.
OF COURSE she came, of COURSE she cursed,
And said: "Clackety-clack-alack-the-day
You ignore me! I'll have my say!
She'll have but three remarks to utter;

The first one: *What's the price of butter?*
Number two: *Has your grandmother*
Sold her mangle yet? The other . . ."
"Stop!" cried Good Fairy thinking fast,
"For *I* shall have the third and last."
(You'll notice how this happens often.)
"I have a wish and I shall soften
This curse; although I cannot change it,
I still can somewhat rearrange it.
So: If your True Love ever finds you,
This awful curse no longer binds you.
The last remark will set you free.
With all my heart is number three!"
The Queen swooned, the King boomed,
But that was that! The child was doomed.
The Princess now is sweet sixteen.
Here she is in our first scene.

(*The* MINSTREL *bows, opens the curtains and then sits at the edge of the stage to watch the play.*

There are two thrones upstage center. On the big one sits the KING. *On the little one sits the* PRINCESS. *Downstage right, facing the audience, is a line of* SUITORS. *Downstage left, facing the audience, is a line of* COURT LADIES. *All of their speeches are said directly front, to the audience.*)

SUITORS. We've vowed our love, our hearts a-flutter,
 And she says . . .

PRINCESS. *What's the price of butter?*

SUITORS. She answers Sultan and Baronet . . .

PRINCESS. *Has your grandmother sold her mangle yet?*

FIRST SUITOR. Emperor . . .

SECOND SUITOR. Earl . . .

THIRD SUITOR. Viscount . . .

FOURTH SUITOR. And King . . .

FIFTH SUITOR. Prince . . .

SIXTH SUITOR. And Duke . . .

SUITORS. We sadly sing.
   We'll flog ourselves, cut off our heads
   And put dry toast crumbs in our beds.
   We'll wear hair shirts and all turn monk
   Ambitions dashed and spirits sunk.

LADIES. A curse is on her. We know not why,
   But to all things she can reply
   In lofty tone or in a mutter
   Only . . .

PRINCESS. *What's the price of butter?*

LADIES. Or with her head at an angle set . . .

PRINCESS. *Has your grandmother sold her mangle yet?*

LADIES. But if she's struck by Cupid's dart,
   She THEN can say . . .

PRINCESS. *With all my heart.*

LADIES. But that remark she will not say,
   Though suitors woo her every day.

SUITORS. We'll wear hair shirts and all turn monk,
   Ambitions dashed and spirits sunk.

 (*In dead-march tempo the* SUITORS *dejectedly file offstage
down right.*)

KING (*rises*). All my nobles you are spurning!
   To monasteries they are turning!
   This silly kind of girlish teasing
   I find, to say the least, displeasing.
   The very next who comes to choose you,
   When on his knees he bends and woos you,
   With all my heart, you answer clear.
   SO I DECREE, my daughter dear!

 (*The* KING *stamps haughtily off down right.*)

LADIES. *"With all my heart,* you answer clear.."
So he decrees to his daughter dear!

(*Ladies laugh and prance off down left. A forlorn* PRIN-
CESS *sits alone on stage. She is crying. After a moment
she lifts her head. She has had an idea. She rises and runs
off down right.*)

MINSTREL (*rising and closing the curtains*).
She'd always done what the King had taught her,
But this was too much for any man's daughter!
She was sixteen and sixteen has pride,
So off she's gone to the World So Wide.
She walked and she walked and she walked all day
To a neighboring kingdom miles away.
As she approached she heard bells ringing
And a dreadful kind of sorrowful singing.

(*Bells are tolling as the* MINSTREL *opens the curtain. He
sits again at the edge of the stage. The stage is bare, except
for a section of wall stage left, with a frightened* PRINCESS
peering over it. As the bells continue to toll, VILLAGERS
*enter stage right in procession as they say their first speech.
As they speak in a monotone, they march single file around
the stage and then form a semicircle stage center. They
repeat their chanting until they are all in position.*)

VILLAGERS. Toll, toll the bells, our King is dead!
He leaves no son to rule instead.
Toll, toll the bells, our King is dead!
Woe, woe, alas; how shall we fare?
Our King is dead and leaves no heir!
Toll, toll the bells!

(*The* IMPOSTOR *enters down left and bows to the* VIL-
LAGERS.)

IMPOSTOR. I happened to be passing by
Just as I heard your doleful cry.

Coincidence beyond a doubt—
I am a King by chance without
A Kingdom. Let all voices ring:
"The King Is Dead, Long Live the King!"

VILLAGERS (*joyfully*). The King Is Dead, Long Live the King!

(*They circle the stage as they shout*)

Tell the news throughout the town!
Spread the crimson carpet down!
Brush the royal purple gown!
Dust the throne! Polish the crown!

(*The* VILLAGERS, *repeating their joyous news, go off right. The* IMPOSTOR, *very pleased with himself, takes stage center and watches the* VILLAGERS *go off. The* PRINCESS *comes around the wall and starts toward him. He turns, sees her, and is petrified.*)

IMPOSTOR. Oh dearie me! It is no guess,
You are a really true Princess!

PRINCESS (*nodding regally*). What IS the price of butter?

IMPOSTOR (*shaking, as he falls to his knees before her*). Ohh!
I beg you not to say you know
That I'm a butterman retired,
Or, Highness, you will get me fired!
For King I may be just as good
As any well-born blueblood would;
So spare a tradesman such disgrace
As being put back in his place!

(*The* PRINCESS *nods graciously and walks offstage left.*)

IMPOSTOR (*rising to his feet, with a great sigh of relief*).
A close call that! But I'm no fool,
And now a butterman will rule!

(*He walks proudly offstage right to the village as the* VILLAGERS *offstage cry: "The King Is Dead, Long Live the King!" and joyful bells ring out.*)

MINSTREL (*closes the curtains and then turns to the audience*).
        And that's how the only ones who knew
        The butterman's trick were I and you
        And the Princess. Let his history
        Remain a fascinating mystery.
        We come now to a forest drear
        And hope she will not venture near.

(*He opens the curtains to reveal a background of dark trees. He shudders and then goes to the edge of the stage to watch.*

  A band of OUTLAWS *slinks in from right in single file. Each is armed to the teeth. They chant their lines in threatening meter with accompanying menacing movement.*)

OUTLAWS. You have read legends old;
        But none of them has told
        Of outlaws half as bold
        As those you now behold.
        For we are more than (*pause—softly*) willing
        To knife you for a (*pause—softly*) shilling!
        This forest is our center,
        And no one dares to enter.
        The neighborhood we terrify,
        The constable we dare defy.
        We look—lurk—loot the land,
        Our Big Bad Bandit Band!

(*The* OUTLAWS *hide behind the trees at the back of the stage.*

  From down left the PRINCESS *wearily enters. She has walked a long way. Her crown is crooked, her cloak is messy, her slippers are muddy. She comes to stage center and sighs. The* OUTLAWS *creep out and surround her.*)

OUTLAWS (*hissing*). Here's a trespasser ripe to strangle!

PRINCESS (*frightened but haughty*). Has your grandmother sold her mangle. . . .

OUTLAWS (*falling to their knees*).
    The password brings us to our knees!
    Our threatening was just to tease!
    Dear Lady, how were we to know
    You came as friend and not as foe?
    And since you bring our countersign
    On milk and honey you shall dine!
    Just wait here beneath this cedar
    And we will notify our leader!

(*The* OUTLAWS *back off right bowing to her. When they are gone, the* PRINCESS *in terror runs off left.*)

MINSTREL (*closes the curtains and turns to the audience*).
    I was frightened to my marrow!
    That escape was far too narrow!
    Thank fortune she had the right words!
    But listen—hush—do you hear birds?

(*There is a gay singing of birds as the* MINSTREL *opens the curtains on a meadow. Across the back of the stage is a row of daisies and buttercups. Above the flowers hangs a round and brilliant sun. The* MINSTREL *smiles his approval and goes to sit at the edge of the stage. The birds continue to sing merrily as a* SHEPHERD BOY *enters right, capering as he plays a penny whistle. He flops down and opens his lunch bag, which is slung on a ribbon around his shoulders. The barefooted* PRINCESS, *without robe or crown, her dress torn and dirty, comes in left dejectedly.*)

SHEPHERD (*looking up at her*). Hello! (*looks again*) HELLO!
    What fun.
    Two for lunch is two times one. (*She hangs her head.*)
    I think your name is Little Bo-Peep,
    And you've lost your tongue as well as your sheep!
    It's cheese and milk and fresh-made bread.
    Too shy to speak? Then nod your head!

(*She gestures to her torn clothing.*)

Yes, I see your skirt is torn;
Your face is dirty; quite forlorn
And underfed and sad you look.
Yonder's what you need (*points off right*)—the brook
Is clear and cold and sweet;
Go wash your face and dip your feet!

(*she goes off right and he calls after her*)

For simple little shepherdesses
With rumpled hair and crumpled dresses
Shouldn't act like fine princesses
Wandering sad in dire distresses.
Just smooth your pretty tangled tresses
And bring us back some watercresses!

(*The* PRINCESS *returns. She looks better and is smiling a little.*)

SHEPHERD Hello! I say hello! What fun.
Two for lunch is two times one.
But you won't talk! Ah me! Ah well!
Maybe you're under a magic spell!
(*She nods vigorously.*)
Well, it really doesn't matter.
Often girls have too much chatter.
But still I'd like at least a word
To know if you have really heard.
(*She smiles and nods.*)
And now that you have found a smile,
I'll treat you with the finest style.

(*He rises and bows gallantly to her.*)

Fair Lady, give me the great pleasure
To grace my feast. Words cannot measure
The joy it gives me thus to greet you.
Allow me, lovely one, to seat you.

(*He helps her to sit. She giggles beautifully.*)

You laugh and milk turns into wine.

(*He gives her a cup of milk.*)

On cakes and pheasant tongues we dine.

(*He gives her cheese and bread. She eats greedily.*
He sits and observes her.)

Now you can't talk it seems; but I
Can, and I will tell you why
You aren't the only one spellbound.
For in these moments I have found
That with no reason and no right
I fell in love at the first sight
Of you. Now please don't think it wrong
For me to use another's song
To tell my love to you, for he
Must have made this song for me.

(*She eats as she listens to his song. Gradually, however,*
she stops eating, and just listens. He strums an imaginary
lute as he sings, and birds twitter an accompaniment.)

"Come live with me and be my Love,
And we will all the pleasures prove
That hills and valleys, dale and field,
And all the craggy mountains yield.

"There will we sit upon the rocks
And see the shepherds feed their flocks,
By shallow rivers, to whose falls
Melodious birds sing madrigals.

"There will I make thee beds of roses
And a thousand fragrant posies,
A cap of flowers, and a kirtle
Embroidered all with leaves of myrtle.

"A gown made of the finest wool,
Which from our pretty lambs we pull,
Fair linèd slippers for the cold,
With buckles of the purest gold.

"A belt of straw and ivy buds
With coral clasps and amber studs;
And if these pleasures may thee move,
Come live with me, and be my Love.

"Thy silver dishes for thy meat
As precious as the gods do eat
Shall on the ivory table be
Prepared each day for thee and me.

"The shepherd swains shall dance and sing
For thy delight each May morning;
If these delights thy mind may move,
Then live with me and be my Love."

(*He finishes the song and takes her hand. He looks at her intently.*)

So say you'll be my love and live
With me. Your answer give!

PRINCESS (*very flustered*). *Has your grandmother* . .

SHEPHERD (*interrupting*). Never fear!
My grandmother's a very dear.
She lives beside the greenwood tree;
I'll take you there for cambric tea.
But don't ask questions just to tease me.
Give me the answer that will please me!

PRINCESS (*in delightful embarrassment*). *What is the price of b* . . .

SHEPHERD (*rising and bending over her*) . . . of bliss?
I think it may be just this kiss. (*kisses her*)
And now I know we'll never part!
Say you'll be mine!

PRINCESS (*shyly, as she looks up at him*). *With all my heart!*
(*They kiss again.*)

PRINCESS. Hello! (*It is a wonderful word. It is her first word!*)

· 144 ·

SHEPHERD. Hello! I broke the spell
        And everything has turned out well!

(*She rises and they stand looking at each other, holding hands.*)

PRINCESS. Hello! (*She looks now all around her. She has never been able to say anything, you know.*)

I say HELLO! What fun!
Birds . . . grass . . . flowers . . . sun . . .
Happiness . . . green . . . gold . . . blue . . .
Sky . . . joy . . . love . . . (*she looks at him*)
. . . you!

(*The MINSTREL softly closes the curtains upon the happy couple.*)

MINSTREL. Their days were full of fun and laughter,
        And they lived happily ever after.
        And all who heard of this romance
        Rejoiced and came to sing and dance.

(*The MINSTREL opens the curtains and joins the entire cast, for everyone is now on stage singing and dancing.*)

PRODUCTION NOTES

This is an elastic play. You can use as many people as you have in your group. If you have a large group, you can use any number of Suitors, Court Ladies, Villagers, Outlaws. If you have a small group, characters who can make quick costume changes can take more than one part; except, of course, the Minstrel and the Princess.

You need only a few stage props to suggest the different scenes in this short play. If you don't have a curtain, the Minstrel can set the stage in plain sight of the audience. If you do use a curtain, the Minstrel really opens and closes it, or pretends to as it is being pulled by an offstage worker.

Two chairs or boxes, a big one and a little one, fancily draped, are the Throne Room. A piece of stone wall, painted on a flat, is the country of the Neighboring Kingdom. A screen or two with cutouts of trees make a Forest for Outlaws. The stage is a Meadow because a big yellow smiling sun hangs above a row of field flowers.

The song the Shepherd sings is a poem by Christopher Marlowe, who lived in the days of Queen Elizabeth I. The costuming should suggest this period. The King and the Suitors wear knee breeches, doublets, ruffs, long stockings and slippers with buckles. Corduroy or velvet jackets belted in make good doublets. White crepe-paper strips gathered on string make good ruffs. Some of the Suitors have short full capes. The King has a long robe and a fancy crown. All of these important, vain men should be dressed elegantly. The Court Ladies are also elegant in long full skirts, padded at the hips, and fancy bodices with high stand-up collars. (Look at pictures of the Elizabethan Court.) The Princess wears a floor-length robe, which completely covers her dress. The dress itself is a simple white low-necked blouse and a full white skirt with a pretty sash. The dress is dirty, torn and messy; the audience does not see it until the Meadow scene. She has a little jeweled crown.

The men Villagers of the Neighboring Kingdom wear knee breeches and belted smocks; the women wear full skirts, blouses, shawls, kerchiefs. The Impostor should be dressed somewhat like a Courtier, but less elegantly. He might have a big hat with a curled feather. Pad his middle with bath towels; he has eaten a lot of butter.

The Outlaws are rather like pirates and are as fierce as you can make them. They have jagged knee pants (cut-off jeans), eye patches, whiskers, kerchiefed heads, bright shirts, and belts brimming with daggers and other savage weapons.

The Shepherd wears knee breeches and a belted smock which is open at the throat. His sleeves are rolled up. Around his shoulders on a strap is his lunch bag. In it is brown bread, yellow cheese, a leather container for pretend milk, a mug. He carries a penny whistle.

The Minstrel is really the master of ceremonies and belongs to no time period. He might wear a modern dress suit (white tie and tails) with a top hat; or he might wear tights and leotard and be like a jester or a Pied Piper. You decide what his character should be, and he must act his part to suit that character.

Offstage you need heavy gongs to strike for the tolling of the bells in the Impostor scene and gongs with a lighter sound for the joyous bells at the end of that scene. In the Meadow scene, use records of bird songs, or have actors offstage play bird whistles.

There are several tunes for the poem "The Shepherd to His Love." Perhaps you can make up one of your own. One of the earliest tunes, published in 1612, is this one:

Come live with me and be my love   and we will
all   the pleasures prove that hills and val-leys
dale and field and all the craggy mountains yield

At the end of the play, the entire cast sings and dances in a fun finale. If it is easier for your group to dance without singing, use a record for the music. A lovely song of the Elizabethan Period is "It Was a Lover and His Lass" from Shakespeare's *As You Like It*. There is a fine Caedmon recording of it in *Songs from the Plays of Shakespeare* by the Shakespeare Recording Society. The music by Thomas Morley appears in *The First Book of Ayres*, 1600.

SOME HELPFUL BOOKS

Berk, Barbara and Bendick, Jeanne, *How To Have a Show*. Franklin Watts, Inc., New York, 1957

Berk, Barbara and Bendick, Jeanne, *The First Book of Stage Costume and Make-up*. Franklin Watts, Inc., New York, 1954

Burger, Isabel B., *Creative Play Acting*. A. S. Barnes & Co., Inc., New Jersey, 1950

Hake, Herbert V., *Here's How*. Samuel French, Inc., New York, 1965

Kase, C. Robert, *Stories for Creative Acting*. Samuel French, Inc., New York, 1965

Lease, Ruth Gonser and Siks, Geraldine Brain, *Creative Dramatics in Home, School and Community*. Harper & Bros., New York, 1952

Leeming, Joseph, *The Costume Book*. J. B. Lippincott Co., Philadelphia, 1938

Siks, Geraldine Brain, *Creative Dramatics*. Harper & Row, New York, 1958

Smith, Moyne Rice, *Plays and How To Put Them On*. Henry Z. Walck, Inc., New York, 1961

Ward, Winifred, *Creative Dramatics*. D. Appleton-Century Co., Inc., New York, 1930

Ward, Winifred, *Playmaking With Children*. Appleton-Century-Crofts, New York, 1947

Ward, Winifred, *Stories To Dramatize*. Children's Theatre Press, Anchorage, Kentucky, 1952

Ward, Winifred, *Theatre for Children*. D. Appleton-Century Co., Inc., New York, 1939